European Issues in Children's
Identity and Citizenship **6**

Growing up in Europe today: Developing identities among adolescents

*Edited by Márta Fülöp
and Alistair Ross*

Children's
Identity &
Citizenship
in Europe

Trentham Books
Stoke on Trent, UK and Sterling USA

Trentham Books Limited

Westview House	22883 Quicksilver Drive
734 London Road	Sterling
Oakhill	VA 20166-2012
Stoke on Trent	USA
Staffordshire	
England ST4 5NP	

2005 © Márta Fülöp and Alistair Ross

First published 2005

British Library Cataloguing-in-Publication Data
A catalogue record for this book is available from the British Library

ISBN-13: 978-1-85856-333-6
ISBN-10: 1-85856-333-X

Designed and typeset by Trentham Print Design Ltd., Chester and printed in Great Britain by Cromwell Press Ltd., Wiltshire.

University of Hertfordshire

College Lane, Hatfield, Herts. AL10 9AB

Learning and Information Services

For renewal of Standard and One Week Loans,
please visit the web site **http://www.voyager.herts.ac.uk**

This item must be returned or the loan renewed by the due date.
The University reserves the right to recall items from loan at any time.
A fine will be charged for the late return of items.

Contents

Series introduction • vii
Alistair Ross

Chapter Synopsis • ix

Chapter 1
**Introduction: Europe as a context for the
development of identity** • 1
Márta Fülöp and Alistair Ross

I Cultural aspects of identity development in Europe

Chapter 2
**The development of social, economical, political
identity among adolescents in the post-socialist
countries of Europe** • 11
Márta Fülöp

Chapter 3
**Multicultural states and the construction of identities:
an overview of the Spanish case** • 41
Maria Villanueva, Concha Maiztegui

Chapter 4
Muslim adolescents in Europe • 55
Louise Archer

Chapter 5
**The identities of youths of Chinese origin: the case
of the British-Chinese** • 71
Becky Francis

v

Chapter 6
**Ethnic stereotypes and prejudice among
Spanish adolescents • 89**
Alejandra Navarro and Ileana Enesco

Chapter 7
**Do history and geography teaching develop
adolescents' historical and territorial consciousness? • 103**
Nicole Tutiaux Guillon

II Identity development and modernisation

Chapter 8
Mass media and identity development in adolescence • 121
Eva Kósa

Chapter 9
**The impact of mediated communication on adolescent's
identity and citizenship • 137**
Jan Mašek

Chapter 10
**The development of consumer identity
in adolescents in Europe • 153**
Victoria W Thoresen

Notes on contributors • 165

References • 169

Index • 185

Series Introduction: European Issues in Children's Identity and Citizenship

Growing up in Europe today: Developing identities among adolescents is the sixth volume in the series European Issues in Children's Identity and Citizenship and is parallel to the fifth volume, *Emerging identities among Young Children: European Issues* (Papoulia-Tzelepi *et al.*, 2005). That collection examines the development of identity during the early years of life – roughly from birth to twelve: this present volume focuses on the teenage years. Together, the two books present a series of analyses, drawn from writers across the continent, about what is different, and what is unchanging, about the way in which children and young people are establishing their identities in the context of a rapidly changing social, political, economic and cultural Europe.

The series has arisen from the work of the ERASMUS Thematic Network Project Children's Identity and Citizenship in Europe (CiCe). This network has brought together over 90 University Departments in 29 European states, all of whom share an interest in the education of professionals who will work with children and young people in the area of social, political and economic education. The Network links many of those who are educating the future teachers, youth workers, social pedagogues and social psychologists in Europe. The CiCe Network began nine years ago, and has been supported by the European Commission's Department of Education and Culture since 1998. It is now completing its second phase of development and planning for a third phase of activities up to 2009.

These volumes have come from our conviction that the changes in contemporary European society mean that we need to examine how the processes of socialisation are adapting to the new contexts. Political, economic and social changes are underway that suggest that we are developing multifaceted and layered identities that reflect the contingencies of European integration. Children and young people are growing up in this rapidly changing society, and their social behaviour will reflect the dimensions of this new and developing social unit. Identities will probably be rather different: national identities will continue alongside new identifications, with sub-national regions and supra-national unions. Our sense of citizenship will also develop in rather different ways than in the past: multiple and nested loyalties will develop, which will be more complex than the simple affiliations of the past. These two books in particular focus on the emergence of identity, and in the present volume, on how this takes place in the critical years between about 12 and 18. At this stage in their lives, young people are becoming very aware of the diversity and richness of their social environment. Their group identities are selected and developed in response to this environment. This book identifies two important threads in this: cultural factors, expressed through the changing and developing ethnic and cultural background of all countries in Europe; and the impact of modernity – in particular, the media, the global economy, and communications technology – on young people.

Those who work with adolescents and young people have a particular role to play in this. They help young people develop their own relationships with the new institutions, societies and technologies that develop, while recognising how different this process might be from that known and understood by their parents and grandparents.

This series is designed to discuss and debate the issues concerned with the professional and academic education of teachers, early childhood workers and social pedagogues. They need to understand the complex issues surrounding the socialisation and social understanding of the young and to be aware of the similarities and differences in professional practices across Europe. They need to work with young people who are learning to be citizens – both of the traditional political entities and of the developing new polities of Europe.

This volume, the sixth in the series, focuses on the development of adolescents' identity. It is thematically linked to the preceding volume on younger children's identity.

CiCe welcomes enquiries from potential members of the Network. These should be addressed to the CiCe Central Co-ordination Unit, at the Institute for Policy Studies in Education, London Metropolitan University, 166 – 220 Holloway Road, London N7 8DB, United Kingdom.

Alistair Ross
Series Editor

On behalf of the editorial committee: Márta Fülöp, Søren Hegstrup, Riita Korhonen, Elisabet Nasman, Panyota Papoulia-Tzelpi, Christine Roland-Lévy and Ann-Marie Van den dries

Chapter Synopsis

Chapter 1: Introduction: Europe as a context for the development of identity

The opening chapter asks what, if anything, is specific to adolescent socialisation in the context of Europe. It identifies the changing context of how young people are socialised in the current context: many of these contexts are global, rather than specifically European. Some defining characteristics are suggested, but these are still tentatitive. Growing up in Europe today is certainly different from how it was in the past. The political and social configurations of the new Europe are such that the new rights to study, work and travel across the continent will probably lead to some significant unique effects, but currently these are not strongly evident.

I Cultural aspects of identity development in Europe

Chapter 2: The development of social, economical, political identity among adolescents in the post-socialist countries of Europe

This chapter gives an overview of the major characteristics of the 'omega-alpha generation', the young people growing up in the so-called transitional societies of Central and Eastern Europe, comparing them to their Western European counterparts. Two basic assumptions are presented: that different socio-political contexts for development lead to different modes of thinking, different values and attitudes, and that growing up in a post-socialist society that is undergoing abrupt change requires a different kind of adaptation than what is needed for the gradual societal change experienced by young people in the traditional democracies and market economies of Western Europe.

The research described shows the fast pace at which conceptions are changing, and that young people growing up in parts of Europe with different histories are increasingly becoming similar. But there are still some characteristic differences, discernable along two cultural dimensions: those of individualism – collectivism and of separateness – relatedness. This chapter also compares differences in attitudes and beliefs such as trust and distrust, attitudes towards control, orientations towards the future, particularly concerning planning and the perspective of time, perceptions of the market economy and competition, beliefs in social justice and hard work, and the roles that money and affluence play in the value systems of young people growing up in the rapidly changing transitional societies of Europe.

Chapter 3: Multicultural states and the construction of identities: an overview of the Spanish case

Globalisation, sustained by the spread of new communication and information technologies, affects the social environment, everyday life and social governance. The development of economic activities on a global scale has modified the relationship between the local and the international, and the rates and scale of exchanges have accelerated. As a consequence, traditional social and cultural patterns are experiencing pressures towards homogenisation: habits of consumption, artistic movements and lifestyles are all affected by the near-instantaneous diffusion of ideas, information and propaganda. Several decades ago a general assumption was held that globalisation would lead to a weakening of nationalistic and regional tendencies. However, as world integration increases we are observing a growing movement to identify with the specificities of territories and localities. This 'return to place' can be represented as a consequence of the tensions between the global and the local and between ethnic fragmentation and homogenisation. This chapter analyses the question of young people's territorial identities in Spain, a multicultural and plurinational state, with particular emphasis on the regions of Catalonia and the Basque Country which, because of their specific features, provide a useful framework for deeper analyses.

Chapter 4: Muslim adolescents in Europe

Muslim identities currently constitute highly topical issues of concern and debate across Europe. Recent world events have heightened popular fears of 'fundamentalist' Islam, and Muslim people are currently subjected to widespread racism and xenophobia. For young first and second-generation Muslim migrants growing up in Europe, the education system often provides a focal point within which dominant fears and injustices are played out, exemplified by the recent French legislation to ban the wearing of the *hijab* in schools. Schools also constitute an important site within which young people construct and generate their identities, and this chapter contrasts popular, simplistic stereotypes of Muslim adolescents with the views of Muslim pupils themselves.

The chapter charts and critiques some popular, dominant social scientific constructions of second-generation Muslim adolescents and proposes alternative, complex and subtle ways of understanding their identity development. Drawing upon research conducted with Muslim young people in Britain, it is suggested that Muslim boys and girls construct multi-layered, gendered, classed and culturally entangled identities which involve the de-/re-configuration of notions of 'culture', 'race', ethnicity, religion and nationality. The chapter aims to assist educators and researchers in the development of less oppressive and more sensitive ways of understanding and engaging with these issues around Muslim identities.

Chapter 5: Asian adolescents' identity in Europe: the case of Chinese in the UK

This chapter analyses the social identities of British-Chinese young people. After a brief history of Chinese migration to Europe generally, and to Britain specifically, background information is given about the current economic and social situation for the Chinese ethnic group in Britain. It then discusses identity as Chinese, noting that some Chinese in Britain have come from Chinese communities in countries such as Vietnam, while others are of Vietnamese parentage but were born in Hong Kong before being brought to Britain. Research evidence concerning young British-Chinese people's outlooks, aspirations and behaviour is explored to provide an overview of the construction of British-Chinese identities.

Chapter 6: Ethnic stereotypes and prejudice among European adolescents

There are significant differences in approaches to integration between different countries in the European Union that relate to their recent history of immigration. For instance, while countries such as France, Netherlands, and the United Kingdom have a long tradition in receiving immigrants, in Spain this is a recent and fast growing situation. This chapter presents a review of studies conducted in Europe, in particularly in Spain, with pre-adolescents and adolescents to analyse their views on topics related to ethnic and racial prejudices.

Specifically, the focus is on research on stereotypes and ethnic-racial prejudices and on attitudes towards ethnic discrimination. Different procedures used by researchers to evaluate these issues are discussed. Though many investigations are substantially very different in their procedures and objectives, the chapter is able to compare the development of prejudice and how adolescents perceive discrimination in diverse European countries.

Chapter 7: Do history and geography teaching develop adolescents' historical and territorial consciousness?

It is generally assumed that history and geography contribute to the formation of collective identity and citizenship, through developing shared representations of the past and of the world, and shared values and acceptance of responsibility for the particular territory and its future. These aims are particularly important for adolescents in constructing their identity (or identities) and in becoming more aware of what it means to act as a citizen. Several research projects suggest that there is a gap between such outcomes and what is really taught and learnt in school; this is illustrated with particular reference to France.

This chapter examines two main concepts used to analyse the intentions and the results of effective teaching and learning: historical consciousness and territorial consciousness. It discusses the relevance of these concepts for history and geography didactics, particularly from the perspective of developing collective identity/identities through teaching and learning these subjects. The French curricula concerning historical and territorial consciousness are briefly analysed. Their objectives are then contrasted with the consistent results of quantitative and qualitative research projects among adolescents, and the discrepancies noted. The effective contents and practices of history and geography teaching in France are the examined: the main conception is still positivistic and teacher-centred. The chapter discusses whether these contents and practices explain the gap between intentions and outcomes.

II Identity development and modernisation

Chapter 8: Mass media and identity development in adolescence

Young people's perceptions of reality, of social norms and of socially accepted behaviour are influenced by their intensive use of both traditional and newer media and their near continuous exposure to mediated representations, popular images and symbolic models. This massive flow of repeated images accumulates and shapes the overall childhood experience, transforming the process of socialisation into a quite different phenomenon from that experienced by earlier generations. Media are a powerful factor in determining what teenagers think about the world and how they define, relate, and perceive themselves in relation to it.

This chapter discusses the role of the media in the development of identity in adolescence from two perspectives. The first of these focuses on the power of the media to model and influence, which is connected mainly with being exposed to the content of the media. The second focus is connected primarily with the context of media use, namely with adolescents' media usage, and with age-related changes in media-related activities, showing how young people actively use media to express and to form an identity.

Chapter 9: The impact of mediated communication on children's identity and citizenship

This chapter introduces and analyses basic aspects of mediated communication and virtual experience in relation to adolescents' identity and citizenship educational environments. The communication technology issues are discussed in the context of the dominant use of computer-mediated communication systems and telecommunication networks to compose, store, deliver and process communication. The limitations of the author's media-model are made clear, as the problems of mediated communication are very complex, but its use allows us to deduce the level of psychosocial quality and social proximity of media systems, especially cyberspace, television and the web, in the social and citizenship communication. The ability to transfer content with features that reflect the emotional and social aspects of humanity and the ability of the media to imitate reality, independently of media content, are important aspects of the impact of media-based environments on adolescents. Educators should not underestimate the role of poorer interactive text-based environments, such as chat rooms, e-conferencing systems, and e-mail, in which adolescents can realise their psychosocial needs and experiment with their identity and sexuality or explore particular social roles.

The third theme of this chapter is how the media support capabilities for citizenship education in the use of media and teenagers' civic attitudes and feelings. In general, young people's social behaviour and citizenship are increasingly influenced by media information resources, citizenship related discussions with software simulations and by producing citizenship related cultural products, such as their own text documents, websites or videos.

Chapter 10: The development of consumer identity in adolescents in Europe

In heterogeneous and market-dominated societies material consumption has become a major indicator of the quality of life. Identities are formed, choices are made and social acceptance is determined to a great extent by the individual's performance in relation to commercial influences. To what extent are the identities of today's European youth formed by the media and the market? Does membership of the 'global teens' (Coupland, 1991) have priority over concepts of identity based on cultural background, language, political opinions, religious affiliation, economic status or locality? Can young people distinguish reality from market-designed images or are they, as researcher Rolf Jensen (1999) claims, dwellers in a 'dream society' in which the 'good story' is the key to success? Do the stories of pop idols and movie stars fascinate youth to the point that they want to adopt their identities and life-styles, or have they acquired the art of discernment and become independent thinkers and active citizens? This chapter examines modern young peoples' identity from both the perspective of social constructivism and of other theories of individual development.

1

Introduction: Europe as a context for the development of identity

Márta Fülöp and Alistair Ross

A dolescence is a formative stage in the construction of identity, as an individual and as a member of a community or communities. One of the most striking theoretical developments in recent years has been the increased emphasis on the importance of context in making sense of social development. The development of identity takes place in micro and macro contexts. For children and young people, the context of development is not only the family, but the geographical, historical, social and political setting in which the family is living. Young people's social development takes place against a backcloth of changing social and political circumstances (Coleman and Hendry, 1999). In this respect, Europe is a social and political context for the development of those who were born and/or who are brought up in this part of the world.

The title of this book is *Growing up in Europe*: several other books and collections have also addressed this topic specifically in relation to adolescence (eg Chisholm *et al.*, 1995; Nurmi, 1998; Alsaker and Flammer, 1999). These and other writers all suggest that there is something unique or specific about Europe in the development of children and adolescents – other than the mere geographic location and context – that makes it important to address developmental changes from this particular perspective. But is there really anything so exceptional about growing up in Europe, compared, for example, to growing up in the USA or in Eastern Asia? Can we identify a distinctive group of young Europeans? In other words, is the social construction of European youth possible? Chisholm (1995) writes of European cultures and societies as dynamic and open networks, living in sensitive interdependence. She argues that this means that there are closer connections between countries, increasing educational and employment opportunities across the European Union, and that each country is increasingly affected by what happens in the others. The question remains: how it is possible to make sense of the complexities of these processes and relate them to the social construction of youth in Europe?

There has not yet been a systematic analysis of what it means to be a European adolescent and young adult. Books that have attempted to introduce this have a kaleidoscopic nature: they do not discuss all countries, or all regions, systematically (e.g. north and south, east and west), but instead present a fragmented picture of different countries, regions and topics.

There have been other efforts to describe systematically young people's social development in different regions of the globe. Larson (2002), an editor of *The World's Youth*, writes that the study of adolescent psychology is an ethnocentric enterprise. A disproportionate number of our images of what happens in adolescence are based on the American and European teenager. There are markedly different adolescences in other parts of the world that must be recognised as different accounts. Following Larson's argument that the Eurocentric view is not universal gives us a better understanding about what, if anything, is distinctive about the European.

In his summary of adolescence in Western countries Arnett (2002) takes European, US and Canadian adolescents together as comprising 'Western youth' because of their many similarities when compared to Asian or African adolescents. He points to the fact that there are very few differences between North American and European young people, the most specific being family relationships. Young European adults tend to live with their parents for longer than do their counterparts in the United States, especially those in southern and eastern Europe (see also Fülöp in this volume). There is also more freedom around sexual behaviour in Europe, less teenage

2

pregnancy, and more violence towards immigrants committed by male peer groups in their late teens. Arnett argues that these differences do not seem sufficient to create a qualitatively different pattern of European adolescence, and therefore the term 'Western youth' is more appropriate.

Tutiaux-Guillon (Chapter 7 in this volume) discusses the research into geography and history teaching in relation to identity building in Europe undertaken as part of a transnational study. She observes that even when national tendencies are apparent, European young people largely display similar shared social representations of the past and views of history – but also that a recent replication of this study made in Canada has suggested that these views may be better considered as occidental and not as a purely European phenomenon.

Such similarities between youth patterns may be seen even more strikingly across large geographic and cultural distances. The lives of middle-class young people in India, South-east Asia and Europe have more in common with each other than they do with those of poor young people in their own countries (Saraswathi and Larson, 2002).

The conception of European youth also depends on the point of comparison. If the viewpoint is North America, then it seems Western European adolescents are closer in similarity to their North American counterparts than to their East European neighbours. For instance, Eastern European adolescents report lower senses of well-being and less optimism than do adolescents in Western Europe and the United States (Grob and Flammer, 1999; Botcheva, 1997; Fülöp in this volume). But if the point of comparison is Asia or Africa, then European adolescents, in whatever region of Europe, are more similar to each other and differ from their Asian and African peers.

To consider adolescents growing up in Europe is to think of a very diverse group of young people. A majority of them are growing up in societies where the social, political and economic structure of society has been relatively stable for a century, but a sizeable minority of young people in the so-called transitional societies have gone through abrupt changes little more than a decade ago. These

3

changes have resulted in these adolescents of East and Central Europe gradually being put on the map of Europe. Social change is occurring in both groups of countries in Europe: in one the process is gradual and slow, related to globalisation, modernisation and the changing role of women and the growing proportion of elderly in the society, while in the other group of societies the changes are sudden and dramatic transformations of economic, political, and social institutions (Pinquart and Silbereisen, 2004).

Thus one very specific feature of European adolescent development is that there are a number of transitional countries that have had to unite with traditional capitalist countries. What is unique about Europe is the socialist/capitalist ideological, economical and political shift and its speed of change. This is a large-scale historical change affecting many millions of young people's lives in Europe, without a parallel in any other part of the world. For this reason many studies focusing on European adolescents identify this feature as distinctively European. .

Chisholm *et al.* (1995) emphasise the significance of this continuing process of transformation in Central and Eastern Europe, which includes the reunification of Germany and the moves towards greater economic and political integration in the European Union. Both have great influence on today's children and young people. Chisholm and her colleagues ask if the childhood and youth research communities are prepared for the problems connected with the emergence of such a 'new' Europe.

But the development of the European Union does offer something rather different in terms of a political unit to which different and novel kinds of attachment might develop. Young people in Europe today are aware, in a way that their parent and grandparents were not, of the possibilities and opportunities of study and work in a range of European nations. This was not a possibility for earlier generations: while the opportunities may not yet be taken up to any great degree, they are nevertheless there and known of. They constitute an entitlement, and a possibility: in that sense they contribute to the imagined community of Europe in the emerging social identities of young Europeans. Statistics are hard to determine, but it is very probably that more young people in Europe today are studying in, working in and travelling to other European countries than at any point in history, and that this phenomena is greater than in any other region of the world – with the significant exception of armies of invasion or occupation. This possibility to travel, study and work is novel, in that it is a right, rather than a privilege.

This volume takes Europe as a wider context for the development of adolescent identity. As with earlier books on the subject, it does not offer a complete representation of growing up in Europe, but rather a collection of different viewpoints, a kaleidoscopic set of varied and colourful moving pictures, of what it means to be a European adolescent.

The first section of the book focuses on cultural aspects of the development of identity in Europe. Fülöp (Chapter 1) discusses the cultural features of young people growing up in the transitional societies of Europe, while Villanueva and Onate (Chapter 2) concentrate on the multicultural issues arising between historically long-standing communities in Spain. As the population of young people in Europe is becoming more ethnically diverse, and issues of ethnic relations between adolescents become increasingly important, we devoted two chapters to the construction of identity of adolescents from new communities in the UK, whose family origin is from outside Europe. Archer writes about Muslim adolescents in Chapter 4 – an area of much contemporary interest – and Francis about Chinese adolescents, who are widely settled not only in the UK but all over Europe (Chapter 5).

Societies such Britain might now be described as having a tradition of multiculturality, and there is much focus on adolescents whose origins lie in other cultures, but this is not the case in seemingly more homogenous societies. In Chapter 6, Navarro and Enesco describe how young people in a traditionally culturally diverse, but not ethnically diverse, society such as Spain perceive and react to minority ethnic groups. They describe adolescents' prejudices and stereotypes towards the Gipsy minority and Moroccan migrants.

This first part of the book demonstrates that growing up in Europe today refers to very different and changing contexts, and that what may be different from earlier generations is that young people are now being socialised to accept and value diversity in cultural background and origins. Adolescents' development of identity across Europe takes many forms and shows great variations.

Cultural distinctiveness and globalisation

Chisholm (1995) observes that young people are inevitably caught in the widening chasm between the global and the local. This is often referred to as the dilemma between homogenisation and differentiation. We explore this paradox in this book, examining two seemingly contradictory trends in Europe: those of cultural distinctiveness and of globalisation and the emerging globalised youth culture, which apparently emerges independent of geographical location, ethnic origin or political history

So the first part of this book examines adolescents in historical and cultural contexts and emphasises cultural differences between different adolescent groups, taking for granted the impact of local culture on the development of identity. However, the second part of the book examines the opposing trend, mainly emphasising how cultural differences are being minimised, among young people in Europe and also among young people worldwide. Three chapters deal with identity development and modernisation: Kósa writes on the mass media (Chapter 8), Masek on mediated communication (Chapter 9) and Thorensen on consumer identity (Chapter 10). Between them, they discuss the processes, means and contexts by which the unique cultural identity of the growing adolescent is surrounded, replaced, or even reinforced by a globalised one.

It may sound paradoxical to ask if there is any specifically European in the globalisation processes induced by media and information technology use and consumption by European adolescents. There are few specifically European characteristics in the content of the media: Kósa suggests (Chapter 8) that the commercial media are both highly globalised and highly Americanised. Thorensen

(Chapter 10) writes that geographical, biological, political, economic and historical factors are no longer key determinants of identity for today's young people in Europe. Joining a common 'youth movement' that is directed by market forces, adolescents unite to emphasise that they are 'the new generation'. In addition, Masek (Chapter 9) points out how the world is shrinking through the new technologies such as the internet that bring people varied parts of the world into close contact with each other. Thus aspects of the media, IT and consumer identity might contribute to the emergence of a global identity of a world citizen, rather than a specifically European citizen.

The effects of globalisation may be somewhat overemphasised and simplified in the literature. Schlegel (2000) writes of the emergence of a globalised youth culture: 'look at your fellow passenger on any train in Europe: if there are adolescents among them, try to guess their nationality. It will be difficult, because young people all over Europe wear the same kind of clothing and style their hair in similar ways' (p 71). But other research shows that Hindu, Muslim, Buddhist, Confucian and Jewish values and beliefs remain intact with modernisation, and that globalisation is not synonymous with Westernisation (Larson, 2002). This is clear in Archer's chapter (Chapter 4), for example in the comments of British-Muslim girls about wearing the *hijab* (headscarf).

Larson (2002) suggests that ethnic identities are becoming more salient in many locales, reflecting individual's reaffirmation of the particularist over the global. Media that have had the greatest globalising effect no longer structure time, daily activities or routines in the homogeneous way that they used to in earlier decades: they now allow various and diverse forms of use and choice, thus contributing to establishing various highly different forms of individuality and to a diversification of lifestyles (Chapter 8). As Brown and Larson (2002) write, there is a selective participation in global youth culture.

Villanueva and Onate (Chapter 3) point to similar processes where, while globalisation de-emphasises nationalistic and regional tendencies and world integration increases, in practice we observe a growing movement against this, to identify with particular aspects of territories and localities. They call this process glocalisation, meaning that young people are defending their own 'place' in order to confront the 'non-place' space that is created by the information era. This is not the development of a globalised identity but of building a localised identity.

Multiple identities

Extending one's identity is the overarching task of adolescence. If there is a distinct category of European youth, then there should also be a well-developed European identity. Our authors argue that the processes of identity-building and self-categorisation have not resulted in a simple and clear-cut European identity. The chapters in this book discuss different types of identities shown by adolescents: regional identity, national identity, religious identity and ethnic identity. These young people show several of these identities: Villanueva and Onate show Basque and Catalan young people having a shared or plural identity, split between the regional and the Spanish.

Brown and Larson (2002) ask if these different identity levels of adolescence create an identity that is fragmented, or one that is rich in complexity. Many of our authors emphasise that identity should not be considered as monolithic or fixed but as contingent: an evolving multicultural and heterogeneous process of construction carried out in interaction with the social environment (see Chapters 4 and 5). Both Archer and Francis adopt a social constructionist view of ethnic identity, demonstrating how gender and ethnicity create a complex and dynamic notion of the self. Many Muslim girls living in the UK have created distinctly hybrid British/English Muslim identities, arguing that they need to define themselves by their nationality and country of birth (English/UK), by their religion (Muslim) and by their gender. British Muslim boys also draw on and construct a range of ethnic, national, religious and popular masculinities in a multi-layered identity.

Thorensen also describes identity as multiple (Chapter 10). She uses a range of possible similes to explore what kind of multiple identities are built in response to the commercial enterprises that invest billions to persuade adolescents to construct identities around their products. For example, she suggests the simile of multiple identities as segmented, like a tangelo, which is a hybrid of a tangerine and a grapefruit, or the alternative of being nested like an onion, lacking a basic or core identity.

In a global world, mass media and communication technologies also strongly influence identities, though there is some dispute as to the direction of the consequences. Kósa refers to two possibilities (Chapter 8). Though the media often function as cultural and social homogenisers, she points to a counter-globalisation effect. Minority groups in many European countries are either underrepresented or missing in the media and may also be portrayed negatively. Adolescents from these minority groups become increasingly frustrated at this social exclusion, oppose the exclusive portrayal of the majority culture, and thus strengthen their attachment to and identification with their own ethnic group.

In our search for distinctive European features of adolescents growing up in Europe we have not been able to find a clear and unique pattern of characteristics that can be specifically identified under this label. However, Tutiaux-Guillon (Chapter 7 in this volume) discusses how history and geography teaching in school can contribute to historical and geographical consciousness, that is, local and European awareness and identity. She uses the expressions 'historical consciousness' and 'territorial consciousness' to identify an attitude or ability to develop social and personal significance that is related to the past and to space: to think of oneself as a historical being, and as responsible for a shared territory, with an identity rooted in a shared past and/or in a shared land, nurturing collective and individual identity(ies). Historical consciousness is awareness of belonging to a group that claims a history, an inheritance, a social memory, and celebration of events figured as a symbolical part of its identity. We began this introduction suggesting that Europe might be no more than a geographical context for young people living in the continent. Tutiaux-Guillion reports that only a minority of 16 to 18 year old students explicitly perceived geographical territory or historical consciousness as the foundation for their identity. Equally she also notes that there are low levels of national or patriotic affiliation. Perhaps this can be related to the greater particularisms of identity that young people appear to be showing towards describing themselves in term of region, ethnic group, language group, gender and religious belief. It is also possible that there is some form of supranational affiliation growing amongst some young Europeans, as described in more detail in some of the contributions to Roland-Lévy and Ross (2003: in this series). One of the issues that emerges from the contributions to this volume is the notion of European identity is probably likely to be *sui generis*, and that we are not sure what it might look like. We probably should not be seeking something that resembles and replaces the national identities of the early 20th century.

I: Cultural aspects of identity development in Europe

2

The development of social, economical, political identity among adolescents in the post-socialist countries of Europe

Márta Fülöp[1]

Adolescents growing up in the so-called transitional societies of Central and Eastern Europe have different experiences from those of their counterparts in those European countries that have not gone through major structural changes during the last 60 years. There are two reasons for such differences. Partly, they are being brought up in a society that had, for many decades, very different guiding principles from those of the traditional, capitalist market economies and democracies of Western Europe. Their parents and teachers were educated and employed in a society that propagated a communist-socialist ideology and in an economy that was mostly state controlled. These differences, in the broader societal system and within the microsystem of the school and family, might be expected to lead to different norms, values and other cultural products in the two groups of adolescents. Secondly, in the post-communist/socialist countries young people are growing up in a period of abrupt social change. Pinqart and Silbereisen (2004) address the developmental psychological question in a recent article: is there a difference between adolescent development in cases of gradual change and in cases of sudden social change? Does the speed and volume of change at the macro level of society – and as a consequence of this, change in the meso- and microlevel environment (Bronfenbrenner, 1979) – have particular effects on the developmental outcomes of these young people, and does it lead to different kinds of developmental paths?

Historical changes in cultural conditions may lead to marked differences in adolescent behaviour between cohorts because of the particular sensitivity adolescents show to changes in their environmental conditions (Baltes and Nesselroade, 1972). Young peoples' lives are touched by all the major social institutions: the family, education, employment and politics. And since young peoples' lives are in transition, they tend to be exceptionally responsive to changes in their surrounding social, economic, political and cultural order.

This chapter identifies certain dimensions of difference currently found between adolescents in Western Europe and those growing up in the transitional societies of East and Central Europe. ('Western Europe' is used here not as a geographical expression, but as a common denominator of those European countries in which democracy and a capitalist economy have been functioning uninterruptedly for centuries, irrespective of their location.) It is hard to disentangle the effects of abrupt social change from the effects of the former socialist/communist society: this requires a thorough analysis of accumulated available data about this group of young people in comparison to their 'Western European' counterparts.

Van Hoorn *et al.* (2000) describe those young people who grow up in societies undergoing structural change as the 'omega-alpha generation' because they are the last children of the old system and the first adults of the new. Adolescents who came of age in the 1990s in the nations of Central and Eastern Europe are historically a unique generation: their adolescence was marked by radical political and economic changes (Macek *et al.*, 1998). These young people are in a double limbo or a double transition (Roberts *et al.* 2000). Their developmental transition from adolescence to young adulthood has had to face, in parallel, both the grave politico-institutional and social changes within the transitional societies and their own transition from child to adult. They are leaving childhood without established adult roles, yet at the same time the society into which they will be integrated is also in transition. The literature on young people in the West is full of metaphors, such as individuals embarking on life's course without reliable maps of what lies ahead, but the conditions surrounding young people in the 'limbo countries' are even less predictable and known.

We should emphasise that while post-socialist societies have much in common, they nevertheless have different histories, cultures and post-communist trajectories. The speed and level of change of those countries that recently entered the European Union is very different from the 'candidate countries' still waiting for accession. There are also differences within these two groups: for example Flanagan *et al.* (1998) found that Hungarian adolescents perceive their school climate as democratic in a similar way to American and Swedish young people, whereas Czech, Bulgarian and Russian adolescents report perceiving their schools as significantly less democratic. This might relate to Hungary having had relatively the greatest degree of political freedom among these countries in the pre-1980 period. Similar differences can be seen in the Western European countries. Although they all developed capitalist market economies and have democratic political systems, there are significant cultural differences between them. For instance, it has been shown that differences between East and West Germans are significantly smaller than differences between both of these groups and other western populations such as the French (Trommsdorff, 1999). Csapó *et al.* (1999) compared three samples of adolescents: Hungarian minorities living in Romanian Transylvania, Hungarians living in Hungary, and Romanians living in Romania. Among the three samples they identified three types of relations. Each relation links two of the three groups and separates them from the third group. Language and culture link the two groups of Hungarians adolescents. Country and citizenship and a common socialist and post-socialist history link the two groups of adolescents in Romania. Non-minority status links the adolescents in Hungary and the Romanian adolescents living in Romania. Their future expectations, daily hassles, coping strategies, well-being, intercultural attitudes, and matters they felt within their personal control were compared. For almost half of the variables analysed, the two Hungarian-speaking samples were similar to each other and different from the Romanian sample. Of the three possible relations, it was language and the culture of origin that provided the strongest links between the two.

Different political pasts – different adolescent development?

The general assumption among social scientists is that the characteristics of the macrosocial environment influence certain aspects of the intrapsychic functioning of people, such as their attitudes and values. Thus, some forty years of socialisation in different socio-political systems should affect the thinking and behaviour of individuals, and should therefore account for some differences between young people growing up in the post-socialist countries of Europe and Western Europe. However, this is a matter of debate, and some analysts have asked if there is really a difference among adolescents growing up in transitional societies and market economies. The best natural experiment, as it is frequently called, is the case of East and West Germany. They shared a history, language and culture before their basic political and economical systems, and their supporting ideologies, diverged in 1945.

Many researchers, such as Oswald and Krappman's (1995) comparative studies of the two Germanies, regularly describe 'astonishing similarities'. This surprise was compounded by findings from longitudinal studies of the transformation process, namely that there was little evidence of substantial change in value orientations (Boehnke, 1999). Oswald attributed this finding to methodological bias, and others to their common language and common culture. Reitzle and Silbereisen (2000) suggest a different possible explanation: they found that different degrees of change in values could be observed, depending on the level of integration into institutional micro-systems. The values of East German adolescents and young adults who had completed school or vocational training after the changes had moved closer to those of their West German peers, whereas almost no change was observed in the values of those young adults who had already finished their education or training. Boehnke (1999) proposes yet another explanation: because adolescents are preoccupied by their specific developmental tasks such as physical maturation, establishing close friendships and preparing for their first job, they may be aware of social changes, but find them less important and relevant to their own lives: they only become important if they can be utilised for their own personal development.

Another argument would be that dissimilarities were to be expected and to be looked for because there has been a need, on both sides of Europe, to emphasise in-group similarities and out-group differences: the social construction of differences and similarities is a typical phenomenon of intergroup differentiation and social stereotyping. As a consequence of this, peoples on both sides of Europe wanted to find differences.

This poses the question: does the nature of the macrosocial level of young people's development really signify in socialisation? Many large scale research projects have attempted to answer this through studies of how the changes in Europe affected young people's development. In Germany in 1991, soon after the unification, the programme *Childhood and Adolescence in Germany Before and After Unification* was established. *Euronet for Research on Adolescence in the Context of Social Change* began in 1992, and was a collaborative effort of research teams from European countries and the United States that aimed at describing perceptions of living conditions in different countries and cultures and at examining the everyday lives of adolescents in each country. *Youth in Changing Karelia* (1995-1997), supported by the Academy of Finland, was a similar project to the German, examining the everyday life, political culture and future orientation of adolescents living in the two different Karelias of Finland and Russia. The Swiss Johann Jacobs Foundation also supported several research projects on the effects of political change on adolescents (including the author's own research).

Society is gradually changing in all European countries, and all adolescents will encounter changing values and norms wherever

15

they are in Europe. But in the so-called transitional societies these general and overall gradual changes are embedded into a more profound and dramatic change in the political, economical and social structure of society. This chapter will try to identify which aspects of these changes influence the development of identity in young people growing up in these countries and will try to focus attention on possible aspects of this process and its results that differentiate and unite these adolescents from their peers growing up in other parts of Europe.

When discussing similarities and differences the particular groups compared are also significant. Rippl and Boehnke (1995) showed in a three-sided comparison that East German young people were more authoritarian than their West German compatriots, but less than similar aged Americans. If this had been only a two-sided comparison, between East and West Germans, then explanations might have focused on the non-democratic nature of East Germany: the three-way comparison suggests that other factors must be looked for because the USA sample were socialised in a democratic country but also showed high levels of authoritarianism.

With this in mind, those cultural dimensions that are traditionally used to characterise cultures and cultural difference will be the individualism/collectivism spectrum (private and public interest) and the separateness/relatedness dimension.

Individualism-collectivism: a rebound effect

The general expectation is that young people and their teachers in the post-socialist societies should be more collectivist and less individualistic in their attitudes than their counterparts in Western Europe, because they have had four decades of ideological emphasis on the collective as opposed to the individual in their countries. But longitudinal research studies suggest that they have managed to catch up with individualism very fast.

Van den Auweele's (1975) comparative study is one of the few that were completed well before the political changes and provides an insight into how differences in mentality arise as a result of social change. His study, carried out in the 1970s in East and West Germany, demonstrated that despite sharing the same culture, history and language, the socialisation in different social systems resulted in different mental sets. East German adolescents demonstrated much more collectivist ideas, while West German adolescents focused their future orientation more on themselves and their personal goals. East German adolescents pursued more social goals, such as establishing social contacts, and focused less on hopes for their own material gain.

In contrast, studies carried out in the last ten years demonstrate that East German young people are similar to former West German young people in terms of individualistic values and materialistic goals. These results suggest that with basic social transitions one should expect to find that significant changes in ways of thinking happen very quickly.

Sverko's (1999) study is one of very few that compared young people living under socialism with young people in a post-socialist society. He compared a sample of university students in Croatia in 1983 with secondary school students and university students in 1993 and 1994. His findings show that while not all values changed, two groups showed very definite change: both utilitarian values and individualistic values increased in importance. Moreover, the post-socialist young people not only reached the same level of individualism that was characteristic of young people in the West, but individualism appeared to be stronger in these countries than it was in countries that had not experienced these dramatic social changes. The social paradigm has shifted quickly.

Crawford and Foster (2001) compared Romanian and English secondary school students' and teachers' discourses on citizenship, while Fülöp et al. (2002) compared Hungarian and English teachers' ideas on citizenship and the good citizen. Both studies point to the same finding. English teachers place much more emphasis on the need to educate pupils to be responsible members of society. Hungarian and Romanian teachers made clear the importance of understanding individual rights. In the Hungarian-English comparison,

English teachers spoke a great deal about the importance of co-operating and behaving in a way that will benefit the community, while this was far less prevalent in Hungarian teaching.

Topalova (2003) compared the post-communist younger generation in Bulgaria with French young people, examining their values and attitudes towards national and European identity. The data was gathered from a standardised interview, including open questions and a test of associations, conducted with French and Bulgarian samples of educated young people. The results showed no significant difference between the two samples in the personal importance of basic life values, but did show differences in preferences of goals and to values related to work. The Bulgarians were more individualistic and materialistic and less socially oriented than the French young people.

The identification of future goals can indicate the extent to which the adolescent identifies with the public interest or the common good. Since the 1970s, self-interest has eclipsed public interest in the goals of young people in many societies (Flanagan *et al.*, 1998). Young people have retreated from politics and civic concerns, commitment to the welfare of the broader community has declined and materialist aspirations have increased. However, the importance which adolescents give to the public interest as a personal life goal when they consider their life and future, and how important it is to do something to help their country and to improve their society, has great significance, because their sense of solidarity with others and their identification with group goals are prerequisites of collective action.

Macek *et al.* (1998) studied the extent of beliefs in the caring nature of the local community and found that Hungarian, Bulgarian and Czech adolescents do not perceive local society as caring. Flanagan *et al.* (2003) found that teenagers from the same three countries had a more misanthropic view of their fellow students when compared to their American or Australian counterparts. They suggested that most students cared only for their friends and looked out for themselves rather than helping others. Bearing in mind that the USA is considered to be country that archetypally socialises individualism, then this attitude of young 15 year olds in the transitional nations of Central and Eastern Europe is quite remarkable. Sinisalo *et al.* (2000) showed that in contemporary Russia noncomformism (individualism) and egoism are typical value positions for young people.

In their Karelian research project, Sinisalo *et al.* (2000) studied adolescents' values. In Russian Karelia the largest group showed security oriented values, but immediately following these were the individualists. Among Petrozavodsk (Russian) adolescents security-benevolence values, representing traditional collectivism, were still dominant, but new liberal values, emphasising individualism, self-direction and stimulation/hedonism were rapidly becoming more significant. Finnish adolescents held universalistic values, connected with the well being of the wider world, far more than the Russians. Among Finnish students honesty and responsibility were ranked as the two most important instrumental values, while the Russians valued these at six and twelve respectively. This shows that while the core values of 'soviet consciousness' were collectivist and supra-individual, today virtually all age groups, and especially the young, show values oriented towards personal life priorities and the care of one's own well being. Individualism, as the antithesis to limitless collectivism, is becoming the core of the new world view and the new value system (Sinisalo, 2000).

This could be considered as a rebound effect. In the socialist system collectivism was the main ideological expectation and people conformed with this to various extents in various countries. After the political changes, the collective goals and the public interest were denigrated and private interests became emphasised as more important than public interests.

Separatedness versus relatedness

Individualism, putting self-interest before the public interest and being autonomous in one's life goals, is prevalent among young people in the post-communist countries but this does not mean that parent-child relationships, or the significance of the family in general, are also the same as in Western countries. The relationships of adolescents towards their family in post-socialist countries can be characterised along another dimension: that of separateness versus relatedness (Kagitcibashi, 2004). Whilst West European adolescents tend to aim for separateness, their East and Central European counterparts are characterised by relatedness. There are also differences in family relationships on a North/South Europe axis, which are not considered here.

In Van Hoorn *et al.*'s (2000) study, the majority of Hungarian and Polish adolescents viewed themselves as members of a close and well-functioning family. In contrast to adolescents in Western European countries, they did not view this stage in their lives as a time when intergenerational conflict might be expected. This was true even among those who talked about disagreements and arguments with their parents. The development of a psychosocial identity appeared to be a quiet process, unremarked by family and friends as being critical.

Puuronen and Kasurinen (2000) found more relationships between Russian young people (18-24) and their families than they did among Finns. Russian young people were still living at home with their parents after the age of 18, not only because financial constraints prevented separation, but also as a result of the emotional needs of both parents and children. The family is regarded as of greater importance by young Russians than it is by young Finns and internal relations within Russian families are closer than in their Finnish counterparts. After the age of 19 a young person in Finland is usually seen as too old to remain living with his or her parents, whilst in Russia almost half of the 20-24 year old group still live in the parental home.

Achievement is traditionally connected with autonomy and openness to change, but Sinisalo (2000) found in Russia that it is more connected to family security and close friendship, in other words, to relatedness. Noack *et al.* (1995) found that after German unification parental unemployment led to increased family cohesion in the East, whilst the opposite happened in the West. Walper and Silbereisen

(1994) compared families in West Berlin and Warsaw and found that changes in family income did not necessarily create stresses in family life or in adolescent development. Loss of family income seemed to contribute to family discord and friction among families in West Berlin, but no such effects could be observed among the Warsaw families. Economic deprivation did not seem to correlate with the mutual support and cohesion among Polish families.

When the leisure activities of adolescents from former East Germany and West Germany were compared there were significant differences in their quality, although both groups rated hedonistic activities as important. When the social context of these activities was examined, East German adolescents preferred family and neighbours, whilst West Germans favoured private organisations and non-family members (Trommsdorff, 1999). In another German post-re-unification study (Uhlendorff, 2004) parents were interviewed in East and West Germany about bringing up children between the ages of 7 and 13, and in particular about their development of social networks. East German parents were more protective and less permissive; this difference can again be partially attributed to East German parents' strong family orientation and intensive kinship relations.

Psychologists of Western societies claim that the importance of parents decreases significantly in adolescence, but Macek and Osecká (1996) showed that a very important and stable part of Czech adolescents' self-definition was based on how they felt that their parents perceived them.

Yet another study, by Flanagan et al. (1998), shows the different ways in which teenagers conceptualise their position in the family. In the transitional societies, and in traditional market economies like Sweden, adolescents are expected to do chores at home, but in western Europe these jobs are more likely to be linked to payment and giving an allowance or pocket money is considered the norm. In the families of transitional societies the adolescent is generally not conceptualised as an autonomous and independent individual 'employee' who gets payments for work but as a family member who carries out domestic tasks for the welfare of the family group for free.

These findings suggest that we are witnessing an interesting cultural phenomenon. In Western Europe individualism is also associated with a growing separateness from parents, whilst this link is not found in Central and Eastern Europe. Although young people in the transitional societies are more individualistic outside the family, they have stronger relationships within the family.

Trust and distrust

From a psychological perspective, trust in the institutions of a democratic state is one of the most important issues of social transition. Social capital – the attributes of a society that enables individuals to cooperate and act collectively – is based on a high degree of interpersonal trust and on trust in public and political institutions. Social capital in this context has the properties of a public good, facilitating the achievement of higher levels of efficiency and productivity (Mateju, 2003).

Macek (2003) explored and analysed how trust was represented in the minds of young people in various European countries, collecting data from the Czech Republic, France, Russia, Scotland and Slovakia. He found that, for young people from the post-communist countries, the meaning of trust is related more to important positive interpersonal relationships and to characteristics of 'others' than to legal norms and basic democratic institutions.

Wilkomirska (2000) studied more than 3,000 15 years olds randomly selected from 200 Polish schools. The respondents were asked to rank their degree of trust in 16 institutions of social life. These Polish teenagers, representing the first generation living in a democratic and independent Poland, had the greatest levels of trust in the Catholic Church: this has been traditionally high on the list in Poland (77 per cent). There is also a relatively high level of trust in scientific institutions (67 per cent) and the media (television 65 per cent; radio 63 per cent). The lowest level of trust – in fact a deep distrust – was shown towards the basic institutions of political life in a democratic society: parliament (44 per cent), the government (35 per cent) and the political parties (23 per cent). Roberts *et al.* (2000) present results that confirm this: they found distrust or cynicism among young people related to democratic politics is higher in Poland than in Britain.

The International Social Survey Programme (www.issp.org) surveyed young people's levels of trust in government in 27 countries. All those European countries which had a long tradition of democracy had higher than average levels of trust, with the exception of Austria. But all participating post-socialist countries, except for Russia, showed a lower than average level of trust, with Hungary being the lowest. Trust as social capital seems to be less available in societies with a recent non-democratic history.

Dependence culture versus enterprise culture

The removal of trade barriers and the growth of the single market within Europe has increased the permeability of national boundaries. Companies are increasing expanding beyond national borders, and many managers are employed transnationally, living and working in cultures other than their own. Participation in cross-cultural teams is becoming more commonplace. Young people living in post-socialist societies, together with young people growing up in the traditional European democracies and market economies, now form the joint workforce of the enlarged European Union. But for the post-socialist societies there is evidently a difficulty in moving from a culture of dependency to one of enterprise (Crawford and Foster, 2001), and from a security society to an opportunity society (Flanagan *et al.* 2003).

Such a shift entails replacing the basic stability of existence that was available for all in the socialist countries towards the opportunities for the individual. This is a process of transition from constraint to choice, and from uniformity to pluralism. In brief, the new social order provides more autonomy, but less security: there is more to gain, but also more to lose. Individual responsibility and agency is emphasised.

Orientation towards control and towards the future are distinct concepts and beliefs that describe how the person relates to their environment. These are now examined, as is the belief in effort and hard work, before we examine more specific aspects of change towards a market economy – the perception young people hold of the market economy, of competition in society, and of the role of money. The following sections examine how these crucial psychological features shift functions in the two groups.

Control orientation

Control orientation is the set of beliefs an individual holds about interrelations and the possible causes of future events. An individual's control orientation is part of a wider socio-cultural context. Cultural values and social norms influence individual goal setting and the subjective experiences of the chances and obstacles in attaining these goals. Resources related to the self, such as perceived control and well-being, may facilitate an adolescent's transition to adulthood. How much do young people differ in their belief about the extent to which they can influence future desirable events (internal control) as opposed to such events being influenced by external factors (external control).

In communist countries it was society, to varying degrees, that took responsibility for planning and programming an individual's future. It might therefore be expected that young people in post-socialist countries would tend to have a greater belief in external control, and focus less on achievements through their own efforts. But the results of research on this are ambiguous. Kasurinen (2000) found that Russian adolescents were likely to show low internal control beliefs and a greater fatalistic attitude than Finnish young people. East Berlin children had lower levels of feelings of agency and control beliefs than West Berlin children (Oettingen et al. 1994). But in 1999 Sydow et al. found no significant differences in the level of control between East and West German adolescents. It was the type of school that the students attended that influenced the participants' orientations towards control: for example, students attending a gymnasium and who aimed to enrol in higher education had greater internal control.

On the other hand, the Euronet Study (Grob et al. 1996), comparing 12 to 18 years old in fourteen countries – former socialist, traditional

Western European and the USA – found that adolescents in former socialist countries reported lower degrees of self-esteem and subjective well-being (perhaps related to perceptions of less security and economic stability) than adolescents living in Western European countries. The same study also found unexpectedly higher levels of control expectancy, perhaps related to the perceived freedoms, and implied challenges, of change.

Future orientation: time-perspective and planning

One of the core aspects of adolescents' evolving sense of self is that they set goals for the future. Behavioural motivation comes from future goals that have been set. One basic motivation is the need for security: this encourages an individual to acquire knowledge about themselves and the environment and the relationship between the two and their future. People want to 'know' what the future will be like in order to resolve uncertainty, and planning and committing to goals reduces uncertainty, providing a sense of being able to control the future (Trommsdorff, 1994). Motivational elements in setting directions for the future include hopes and wishes, fears and concerns, an individual's belief that they are in control, and an affective evaluation of the future in terms of optimism and pessimism.

Planning behaviour is therefore generally considered to reduce anxiety; but studies show that Hungarian young people who had a well-structured plan for their futures had higher levels of anxiety, contrary to expectations (Vári-Szilágyi and Solymosi, 1999). This might be explained by the characteristics of their society: planning ahead in an environment that is changing rapidly and sometimes unpredictably means there is a high probability that the plans cannot be achieved, leading to anxiety. A rapidly changing environment it is not the place for a long-term perspective, and short-term thinking is probably better.

Short-term perspectives in transitional societies may also be seen in understanding of the past. Van Hoorn et al. (2000) studied Hungarian and Polish adolescents, and found that they concentrated more on the present than the past or the future. For example, they were only able to discuss social transitions within an extremely limited historical framework, giving little consideration to the near past (their parents' lives) or the near future (their own prospects).

Comparisons of East and West Germany show that when the initial culture was the same, both the acculturation process and the change of intrapsychic functioning between different cohorts can be very fast. In 1994 East German adolescents had fewer expectations for their future lives: they focused on concrete tasks in the near future, showing their shorter time perspective. This was also found with adults from former East Germany: indeed this future orientation factor was the only stable difference between the two former countries at that time (Trommsdorf, 1994; Jülisch, Sydow and Wagner, 1994). A study conducted five years later (Sydow *et al.*, 1999) found no important differences among the two German groups in respect of their views on the future. In Germany there is a common view that the period of transformation is now completed, and few differences remain between West and East Germany. Comparisons of North and South Germany may now account for more difference than comparisons between East and West Germany (Trommsdorff, 1999).

Adolescents' beliefs about social justice and hard work and effort

American social psychology documents a common 'belief in a just world' – that the successful have earned this, and those who suffer deserve this (Lerner *et al*, 1978). This would lead to noting human value if one sees success, and human weakness if one sees failure. But this phenomenon is not the case in East Europe. Security-giving and self-protecting reasoning differs between the well-developed market economies and the post-socialist countries (Hunyady, 2001; 2002). Under the communist/socialist system, all members of society received social support, regardless of their level of contribution to the society. Individual rewards did not depend on individual effort ('from each according to ability, to each according to need'). In practice, advancement had less to do with hard work and dedication than it did to political connections, and was based on subjective – and often political – assessments. Part of the transformation to the market economy aimed at eliminating this disjunction between individual effort and economic reward.

Smith, Dugan and Trompenaars's (1996) study suggested that, in terms of organisational management, the major cultural divide lies between Eastern and Western Europe, rather than between the other geopolitical regions of Europe. West European countries from the Nordic, Anglo, Germanic and Latin European clusters tend to score higher on work-related values towards 'equality' or 'egalitarian commitment', showing that achieved status is valued more highly than ascribed status. For example, work is perceived to be evaluated fairly, and there are reportedly objective criteria for making appointments. On the other hand, Central and Eastern European countries (including the former East Germany) tend to score higher on 'hierarchy' or 'conservativism', showing that ascribed status is valued more highly. Power differentials, paternalism and nepotism are reported as expected or accepted.

Flanagan *et al.* (2003) compared the views of young people from six nations selected to represent two types of societies: security societies and opportunity societies. The first group (Bulgaria, the Czech Republic, Hungary and Russia) were categorised as security societies because for forty years the state had guaranteed citizens' basic needs. Justice was based on the principle of equality of outcomes. In the opportunity societies – Australia and the USA – liberal or private market principles were in place, and the state played a relatively minor role in regulating the economy. Equality of opportunity, or 'a level playing field', was the foundation on which individuals proved their worth. Justice was based on principles of equity (that is, rewards such as income or status are fair because they are earned by effort). Consequently differences in status reflected individual differences in performance. Teenagers from the opportunity societies, working class teenagers and boys were significantly more likely to believe in meritocracy (that an individual's hard work gets him/her ahead) than were teenagers from the security societies, middle class teenagers and girls. Young people in the security societies were also more likely to expect governments to provide welfare programmes.

Fülöp, Roland-Levy and Berkics (2004) compared the views of Hungarian and French adolescents on competition in the market economy. A majority of the French sample agreed that competition in economic activity or in other aspects of life rewards the persistent and hard working (69 per cent, compared to 29 per cent for the Hungarians). They agreed more with the statement that entrepreneurs work hard to achieve success. In contrast, more Hungarians agreed that competition rewards the strong but not the weak (40 per cent, with no French respondents agreeing with this). French teenagers showed a belief in meritocracy, while Hungarians took a more social-Darwinist view. When asked what they considered the most important characteristic of competition, 60 per cent of French students selected 'the effort is more important than the result', while 57 per cent of Hungarian students selected 'the final result is more important than the effort'.

Roberts *et al.* (2000) found very similar patterns among young respondents in the post-communist countries of Armenia, Georgia and the Ukraine. Only a quarter of them believed that hard work was necessary to become rich in their countries. They did not believe that rewards followed ability and effort.

There are however some differences between the post-socialist countries: Macek *et al.* (1998) compared adolescent's views of 'the social contract' in Bulgaria, Hungary and the Czech Republic. In Bulgaria and the Czech Republic they appear to have adopted a basic premise of capitalist society, that individual initiative will be rewarded. This was not the case in Hungary. Young people at the older end of the scale in all three countries were less likely to believe in the value of initiative and were more disillusioned.

Perceptions of the market economy and competition in the new economies

Young people in the post-socialist countries are divided in their ideas about the market economy and competition. They are partly pro-reform, rejecting socialism and preferring capitalism and the market economy: on the other hand, they believe that socialism gave many important and valuable securities that they would like to have back.

It seems that the ideal for most would be a combination of aspects of both the old and the new: the security and social services of socialism and the consumer choice and productivity of the market (Roberts *et al.* 2000).

Vári-Szilágyi and Solymosi (1999) examined the views of Hungarian university students and young professionals (economists, agricultural engineers and architects) on the processes of transition to a capitalist society. They reported a kind of 'ideological limbo', rejecting the old system but not clearly committing to the principles of the new. They agreed that the most important features of a well-functioning society were free economic competition, market-led economic processes, and significant income differentials; but they also wanted full employment and for the state to care for the weak. This combines capitalist and socialist principles: young adults would like the advantages of capitalism without losing the social security provided by socialism.

During the years of transition young people have gradually learned more about the principles of the capitalist economy and understood more about how it functions. Van Hoorn *et al.* (2000) studied young Hungarians and Poles, aged between 16 and 18, to find how their development of identity was connected with societal change, and how they understood and responded to the new socio-political concepts related to these changes, such as the free market economy. The studies took place between 1991 and 1995, and over these four years there were changes in students' knowledge of and attitude towards economic changes in their countries. At the beginning of the period, most had difficulty in responding to questions about the market economy, because their knowledge and understanding was very limited. They found it difficult to distinguish between democracy and the free market. By 1995, young people of the same age appeared to have a deeper understanding of the political and economic concepts of the market economy and its underlying processes: for example, that price is determined by supply and demand. In the later period they applied these new concepts to their own lives: constructing new meanings takes time and experience, and the learning process is gradual.

A study of Hungarian adolescents in 2001 suggested they had a generally positive view of the introduction of the market economy: they emphasised its positive effects on development in Hungary and saw entrepreneurs as the driving force of the economy (Fülöp and Berkics, 2002). But in 2004 Fülöp, Roland-Levy and Berkics were still finding that French adolescents had a more structured and agreed understanding about the role of competition in a market economy than Hungarian students. The French students saw more clearly the relationship between competition and prices, and understood how competing companies might merge to dominate the market.

In parallel with this gradual development of understanding the competitive principles of the market economy there has been a growing disillusionment about its concomitant effects. In almost all post-socialist countries researchers have found that while young people initially welcomed the competitive market, they then began to realise that it was leading to large disparities in income. They felt that this income gap did not necessarily reflect merit or talent, but sometimes was the consequence of private connections, corruption and illegal ways of getting resources. They therefore became less certain about how the market economy might bring them advantages. For example, young Bulgarians had positive attitudes in 1992, but then became less positive about the characteristics of those who were enterprising, rich and economically active (Botcheva, 1998). Similarly, while young Armenian, Georgian and Ukrainian respondents expressed a preference for the market economy in principle, they were cynical about the practices of the market systems that had developed in their own countries (Roberts *et al.* 2000). The examination by Macek (2003) of adolescent perceptions of economic and social changes in the Czech Republic, Hungary, and Bulgaria explored beliefs about the efficacy of individual initiative and hard work. Adolescents in the Czech Republic were the least cynical about the economic changes, while Hungarian adolescents were least optimistic about the future.

In theory, competitive market economies and political pluralism should offer the optimal motivation to develop individual capacities and abilities, and this should differentiate people solely on the basis of their achievements. This should mean acceptance that there will be winners and losers and of the principle 'let the better win: this is how we will progress'. However, if there is a perception that competition is unfair, that immorality wins, and that success is attributed to cunning and nepotism and not to hard work, then there will be negative attitudes towards winners, the successful and the wealthy (Fülöp and Berkics, 2003).

From this one concludes that it is not only difficult and takes time for young people to understand these new political and economical concepts, but that establishing a reasonably positive attitude towards them is not easy. Social cynicism, the belief that the goals justify the means and the lack of reward for hard work and effort are perceived as problems in many of the post-socialist countries by all generations, including parents and teachers.

Competition

Continuing political changes in the former socialist countries over the last decade include the appearance of political pluralism, market economies, unemployment and competition in the job market, and a growing number of enterprises that require a competitive spirit. All of these have resulted in competition – a phenomenon previously banned and denied – becoming a key aspect in these societies. However, there is some confusion about the personal, interpersonal and moral requirements and consequences of competition in this new and harshly competitive environment. This is in part due to a lack of explicit and well-structured principles or rules to govern competition, and in part because people have not been prepared for the emotional consequences of open competition. The transformation to market economies in former European socialist countries has changed the personal and social skills necessary for success. Being able to compete, standing up to losing, and withstanding the stresses of competition are now needed in transitional societies. The rapid changes at every level in post-socialist societies requires individuals to modify their perceptions, understanding, attitudes and values (Fülöp, 2002).

Competition has a long history in the Western capitalist democracies. Fülöp (2002) compared English and Hungarian teenagers' perceptions of the role of competition in their society. While in general both Hungarian and English respondents saw competition as playing an important role in their society, there were qualitative and quantitative differences in their views. For instance, while large groups of English and Hungarians had neutral attitudes towards competition, they expressed this in slightly different ways. The Hungarian neutral answers showed an acceptance of the inevitable: 'Hungary must compete in order to....' or 'We must compete for...': competition was seen as unavoidable rather than naturally present. The English students in the neutral group took competition for granted, not as an outside constraint, but an inherent, self-evident characteristic of a capitalist society.

Those Hungarians who were not neutral were very largely negative towards competition. They gave the fewest positive and the biggest number of negative evaluations about the role of competition, and also had less structured views about the positive consequences and advantages of competition, and a considerably more structured picture about the disadvantages. In contrast the English who were not neutral were five to one more likely to see the role of competition as purely positive. They were more willing to explain their positive, than their negative attitude: they had a less critical attitude towards competition.

Asked to identify the main positive consequences of competition, Hungarian students suggested motivation, the development of the economy, and the country. The British responded that most important was the development of Britain, showing strong patriotic feelings and concern for the welfare of Britain, sometimes even to feelings of superiority over other nations. British students also mentioned motivation and emphasised how competition could lead to self-improvement.

Unlike the English adolescents, Hungarians concentrated more on the negative consequences of competition. The most frequently described consequences were immorality, interpersonal conflict and aggression, and the development of money-oriented people. Hungarians want to win at any cost, particularly in the material sense, and by any means aggressive or immoral. In this new democracy and market economy there are no well-established rules to control competition: the disintegration of the former social rules resulted also in the disintegration of classical moral rules. Interestingly, the inequality created by competition is a greater concern for the English than immorality. Being money-oriented was never mentioned by this group, perhaps partly because it is seen as a natural, rather than a negative, trait, and partly because it is less a sign of being greedy than of being naturally concerned about finances.

When Fülöp and Berkics (2003) compared English and Hungarian adolescents' reactions to winning and losing, the expectation was that English young people between 16-18 would be better socialised towards competition and coping with its potential positive or negative outcomes, because of their cultural, historical, economical and political background: the results confirmed this. Hungarian young people gave great significance to winning and were enthusiastic about this, but were demotivated, sad and depressed about loosing, and were less able to cope with this than their English counterparts. The English respondents took winning as a natural outcome of competition, and confidently attributed it to being 'the best' or being 'better than others'. They were also more activated by losing (being disappointed but 'standing up' to it) than were the Hungarians, so fewer of them expressed explicitly negative views about over losing. Hungarian young people showed paradoxical and ambivalent emotional reactions, both to winning and to losing, and this reflects the different societal context for winners and losers in Hungary and Britain. Hungarian young people tended to be happy about winning, but with a tendency to hide this feeling from others. The English appeared socialised to not show their negative emotions on losing, and this social norm does not appear among the Hungarians, where negative emotions on losing are acceptable. This creates a paradox in Hungary: striving to win, but when this is achieved it is not socially accepted; trying to avoid losing at any cost, but being better socially accepted as a loser.

While English teenagers generally did not associate competition with immorality, when Fülöp, Roland-Levy and Berkics (2004) compared French and Hungarian young people studying economics, both groups expressed equally strong doubts that everyone in a market economy observes the moral rules of business. This indicates disillusionment and social cynicism about the morality of the business world. Both groups agreed with statements that reflected the socialist ideology that had been explicit in Hungary but were not dominant in France, such as that business people get rich at the expense of others and they exploit those who are working for them, and the market economy is beneficial only for a minor group of society. For all three items, there was no significant difference between the two groups. This shows that a rather negative and disillusioned view of the morality of the business world is held by both Hungarian (and other post-socialist) teenagers and by French teenagers growing up in a traditional market economy. This suggests there may also be differences in attitudes between young people towards competition within West European countries such as England and France.

The role of money
In a free market economy the relative income equalities of the socialist system turned into huge inequalities in the post-socialist phase. Money, which had been ideologically unacceptable as a motivator for human behaviour, now became the key force in most areas of life, gaining priority over other values. Material values such as money were already beginning to be important in Belarus in the 1980s, but these doubled in significance in the 1990s after the political changes (Titarenko, 1995). Studies in Russia, Estonia and Bulgaria suggest that in the 1990s young people's main pragmatic and work-dominating value was earning a lot of money, even if this was not their main goal in life (Roberts *et al*, 2000; Yordanova, 1995).

Puuronen and Kasurinen (2000) compared the importance of different aspects of life for Russian and Finnish young people: Russian young people rated achieving a good financial status almost as highly as they did family and friends, and rather more than education, while all three were accorded higher priority by the Finns.

Hungarian adolescents considered money as the main goal of competition in their society, compared to their English peers for whom this was only sixth most important area, after areas such as sports, competition for good jobs and education (Fülöp, 2002). This was supported by the study of Saris and Ferligoj (1995), who found that social contacts were more closely related to general life satisfaction than finances in Western Europe, whilst in most of the East and Central European countries finance was most strongly associated with general life satisfaction. This supports the view that in West European countries satisfaction with social contacts is much more important than satisfaction with one's financial situation, the reverse of the case in Central and Eastern European countries.

One explanation of this phenomenon is that competitiveness and attitudes towards money are inversely related to comparative gross domestic product (GDP) but positively related to economic striving and resulting growth. Furnham *et al.* (1994) argues that once economic wealth has been secured, being money-oriented becomes less prevalent.

However, the importance of money is not only related to the economic output of the countries, as was found in a study comparing Hungarian and Columbian young people. Perez (2004) found that Hungarians were far more preoccupied with money in their thinking about future work when compared to Columbians, even though Columbia is the poorer country. The higher stress on the importance of money is more related to the preceding equality-oriented society, where differences in income and wealth were politically unacceptable.

In a study of East and West German adolescents and their families, Noack *et al.* (2001) found that the financial situation of the family was a determinant of perceived uncertainty in society, and in positive or negative perception of social change. This suggests that it may be that the distribution of financial resources plays a major role in adapting to economic change, and that it is easier for those who have enough money. Resource-poor individuals will probably follow the old developmental paths, whereas resource-rich individuals can be expected to take up the new opportunities. This would suggest that the increase in the levels of preoccupation with money among adolescents in the former Eastern block may be adaptive.

The paradox of goals and esteem

Putting together the fact that having more money is considered a main aim in life with the fact that when one gets rich one is looked on with suspicion and envy, we observe the paradox of wishing for something that will cause condemnation. A situation like this might lead to unexpected self-evaluation and national evaluation.

Mlicki and Elmers (1996) compared Dutch and Polish young people's national stereotypes and national identification. *Social Identity Theory and Self-Categorisation Theory* (Tajfel and Turner, 1979) suggest that when people identify as members of a social group they are motivated to distinguish the group positively from relevant comparison groups. As Polish young people were found to have a more negative national stereotype than the Dutch subjects, it was expected that their identification with Poland would be less strong than the Dutch identification with the Netherlands. But the contrary was found: Polish young people identified more with their nation, despite their negative view of it. This shows a crucial cultural difference in terms of inner functioning and introduces an explanatory principle: Jost and Banaji's *System Justification Theory* (1994) demonstrates how low status group members tend to accept and justify their relatively low status compared to other groups. In Anglo-American culture, young people are socialised to identify with groups they consider positive, as this leads to high self-esteem. However, this might not be the case with countries in Central/ Eastern Europe. Negative national characterisation can be associated with strong national identity, so a person is strongly attached to a group that has negative connotations, leading to a deficit in self-esteem.

The low self-esteem and low national esteem of young people in East and Central Europe was associated with their evaluation by their Western peers in a study by Flanagan and Botcheva (1999). They presented young people with a list of ten countries participating in a cross-cultural study and asked them how much they would like to have contact with people in each of the following countries: Bulgaria, the Czech Republic, Hungary, Poland, Russia, Finland, France, Germany, Switzerland and the USA. Regardless of their national origin, there was a common western bias underlying adolescent preference patterns, with a hierarchy on both sides of Europe about which nationals were seen as most worthwhile to meet. This result is perhaps predictable, given that young people growing up in transitional societies are changing towards the values of the West more than *vice versa*. In German unification, for example, it was Easterners who made more adaptations to the new circumstances, whilst Westerners did not feel the need for change (Silbereisen and Youniss, 2001).

Conclusions

If we summarise the overarching characteristics found among post-socialist young people we can see which elements can be attributed to growing up among rapid social changes and which to the socialist/ communist past. We can also identify characteristics that have changed quickly, and those that have been more stable. For example, the excessive individualism of these young people and their focus on self-interest rather than on public or community good can be attributed either to the extreme speed of the acculturation process or to the former political system having failed to instil the principles of the collective: when the political system collapsed, the true nature of the people manifested itself with greater intensity.

The German example demonstrates this, as within little more than a decade most differences between East and West German young people have disappeared, the commonest explanation being that the communist political system could not over 40 years over-ride the original common culture.

While individualism became prevalent, closer family ties and relationships are basically unaffected by the transformations: these cultural features change very slowly.

Short-term thinking is an adaptive reaction to a rapidly changing environment, in a situation where careful forward planning would lead to frustration rather than control over what happens.

Orientation towards money and striving to be rich is a logical consequence of the previously emphasis on the principle of equality and of the new opportunities opened up by the capitalist economy. Those who are affluent are better buffered against the negative consequences of an unpredictably changing social and economical environment.

Social disillusionment and cynicism about the value and rewards given for personal effort and hard work, lack of trust, and negative views of the rich and the role of competition are partly the result of the non-meritocratic nature of the former system, and partly due to the reality of new market economy practices in the post-socialist countries.

Having fewer skills of coping with winning and losing is a direct consequence of being brought up by parents and teachers unaccustomed to handling competitive situations.

Lower life satisfaction ratings, lower self-esteem and lower national pride are partly because the 'omega – alpha' generation live in societies much less affluent than their Western counterparts and are expected to learn from them and change direction towards them, rather than *vice versa*. Broadening one's outlook and being able to make more social comparisons during the transition to democracy can have negative effects on some young people's self-esteem and well-being.

Culture is a slowly changing entity but the acculturation of young people is very fast. For many young people in Central and Eastern Europe changes in society have been accelerated by the recent expansion of the European Union. Characteristics described here might no longer exist within a decade. Nevertheless, it seems the enlarged European Union will have to live with some degree of diversity in young people's attitudes for the foreseeable future. The more we know and understand these potential differences, the more effective the management of current and future diversity will be: it is the challenge to future social research to tap into this process systematically.

Note

1   The author would like to express her gratitude to the Johann Jacobs Foundation, Switzerland, the Hungarian National Research Board (T 029876), the British Council and the Hungarian Scholarship Board for supporting the researches referred to in this chapter.

3

Multicultural states and the construction of identities: an overview of the Spanish case

Maria Villanueva and Concha Maiztegui

World integration and the renegotiation of territorial identities

The process of globalisation, sustained by the spread of new communication and information technologies, is affecting the social environment, everyday life and social governance. The development of economic activities on a global scale has modified the relationship between the local and the international, and the rates and scale of exchanges have accelerated. As a consequence, traditional social and cultural patterns are experiencing pressures for homogenisation: habits of consumption, artistic movements and lifestyles are all affected by the near instantaneous diffusion of ideas, information and propaganda. The growth of this new society is redefining the role of our centralised social structures. Because production and consumption are operating on a global scale, new structures are required that challenge the rigidity of current state limits. State sovereignty is still a basic element of the international state system but has partly been displaced by other institutional arenas. Common markets and political communities are taking over some state competencies and relationships are being restructured, not only between state and state, but also between society and territory (Sassen, 1996).

The fragmentation of state sovereignty into different agents as a consequence of globalisation has been analysed by different authors (Harvey, 1989; Giddens, 1991). Some decades ago there was a general assumption that the process of globalisation would de-emphasise nationalistic and regional tendencies. However as world integration increases we are observing a growing movement to identify with aspects of territories and localities. Cultural and linguistic minorities are emphasising their identity and claiming for territorial recognition, although in many cases their territories have no definite borders. They represent this 'return to place' as a consequence of the tension between the global and the local, and between ethnic fragmentation and homogenisation. In an attempt to articulate this relationship between global and local, and to avoid the widespread tendency to regard local and global as polar types, some authors use the composite term *glocalisation* (Robertson,1995).

Territorial identities are reappearing at a time when physical space seems to lose its substance and when the idea of the network is replacing the concept of the frontier. Their presence in a globalised world could be considered as a new paradox: the claim for difference running in parallel with the need for integration. As many sociologists conclude, new social movements against globalisation are essentially identity-based: they are defending their 'place' in confronting the 'non-place' spaces created by the information era. The process of creating territorial identities is not only an individual process, but is also collective, and is associated with specific geographical and cultural space (Nogué and Vicente, 2001). Humans create spaces and give them meaning. The place of origin confers identity to the individual and to the group. However, if they move to another space, this will also influence their identity, in different ways. In a global world, mass media and communication technologies also strongly influence identity (see Kósa in this volume) and may also help change the ways in which people identify themselves with a territory. As a result of these multiple interactions, identity should not be considered as monolithic but as an evolving multicultural and heterogeneous construction.

Adolescents have a pivotal role in this process, since identity issues have long been regarded as crucial for young people's development. According to a 1998 United Nations Development Programme report, market researchers created the concept of 'global teens' to describe the urban adolescents who follow similar patterns of world-wide consumption in areas such as music, films and fashion (Jensen Arnett, 2002). There is no doubt that their culture will be affected by the extent they have been affected by global trends. However, in many places regional, ethnic and religious identities have become more explicit. This chapter analyses the question of territorial identities in Spain, with particular emphasis on Catalonia and the Basque Country which, because of their specific features, provide a framework for deeper analyses. General findings of several empirical studies with samples of Spanish young people are presented in an historical and social framework.

Frontiers, national states and the question of territorial identities

Cultural matters are basic to identity and the roots of identity can only be understood in an historical context (Royle, 1998). The consolidation of nation states over the previous two centuries required clear definitions of limits, accurately mapped and internationally recognised. In the 20th century, and for the first time in history, all the inhabitants of the world were living *inside* a map, in well-bounded territories. In every country, the *elite* built an economic frontier against their neighbours and created the structures to substitute the ideology of the old regime with a new internal cohesion, which was sustained by the economy and into spreading the provision of schooling. The rise of nation state was linked to romantic notions of the mysticism of place and to feelings of belonging and not belonging: national identity cannot be considered an immutable entity but as a socially constructed narrative (Graham, 1998). It implies the cultural homogenisation of their citizens, giving them an exclusive identity: the state was conceived of as internally homogeneous in terms of shared cultural content, and this was a means of controlling diversity while adding a further layer to identity (Edye, 2002).

This was achieved through spreading a common language, national feelings and basic concepts and values of a common culture (Hobsbawm and Ranger, 1982). Schooling was a powerful instrument in promoting the language and national feelings. But this process left in its wake cultural, linguistic and national minorities, all over Europe, who had not succeeded in creating their own state structures. Language is the clearest sign of belonging to a particular culture and also constitutes a strong element of personal identity. Behind this is a complex system related to a human group with a common history, traditions and values (Villanueva, 2004). The European mosaic of languages is a clear demonstration of the non-homogeneous nature of European nation-states; many countries are still culturally plural, and it can be said that the majority of European states are multicultural, although school systems have tended to provide for a monolingual national society (Reid, 1999). Territorial identity is a complex concept, a difficult and elusive entity, because it is as much the product of external forces, such as the differing policies and traditions of the central administrative state, as it is of internal factors such as language and culture (Royle, 1998).

The space and identity of states has been changing through history and different political units have appeared and disappeared. The geopolitical changes of the last decade have contributed to a better understanding of these issues. Over the last two centuries the western world used to consider identity as an object, bounded in time and space, and held the idea that sovereignty over everything was bundled into territorial state parcels. However, notwithstanding the importance of states within European thought, they have often been fragile and facing continuous transformations; the reshaping of borders as the result of successive wars seems good evidence of this. The current waves of migration are accelerating the creation of a multiplicity of identities, although this multi-identity dimension of the European population is not without its contradictions and tensions (Nogué and Vicente, 2001). The state remains the main spatial framework but as European integration shows, the political control of space is being renegotiated in a process which is qualified by Graham (1998) as one of re-territorialisation.

Spain as a plurinational state: territory and identities

Modern Spanish society is the result of historical processes that left different languages and a great regional diversity, which constitute an example of a multicultural society. The early settlements of the Greek and Roman civilisations were followed by seven centuries of Arabic influence. Jews, Muslims and Christians were living in Spain for centuries, in a rich intercultural way, through not without tensions. Other people from European regions established themselves in the territory, as did various ethnic minorities such as the gypsies. As a result of this historical mixing, the political borders of Spain today contain diverse identities and four main languages.

The Spanish Constitution (1978) created seventeen Autonomous Communities, many of them rooted in former kingdoms, with a Statutory Law and Parliamentary rule in each of them. These Autonomous Communities are the main political units within the Spanish State. The official language of the state is Spanish but there are three other languages which are spoken in certain of the communities: Catalan is spoken in the communities of Catalonia, Valencia, Aragon and the Balearic Islands, Basque in spoken in the Basque Country and Navarre, and Galician spoken in Galicia. In three of these communities, Catalonia, the Basque Country and Galicia, their history and language have given them a strong identity. Their specific status as nationalities inside a state was not recognised during the regime of the dictatorship (1939-1975) and their formal expression was suppressed. The democratic constitution, which recognised the plurality of the state, helped to consolidate pre-existent identities, which received channels and spaces for their expression. Nevertheless, there are still some tensions and misunderstandings between state and minority cultures.

A 2001 survey, focusing on values, undertaken in Catalonia (Orizo and Roque, 2001) shows a general agreement about the acceptance of Spain as a country in which different identities should be recognised and respected (73 per cent): only 19.5 per cent of the sample replied that Spain should be considered homogeneous and having a single unique identity. In spite of this, 47 per cent of the sample also thought that there was a common identity, shared by all citizens of the country.

The territorial belonging of Spanish youth

The image of territorial belonging in Spain is not uniform: on the contrary, diversity and heterogeneity clearly exist. The research carried out by Moral and Mateos (1999), working with a sample of 2,500 young people aged 15 to 29 and selected from all regions of the country, provides an extensive and broad panorama on this subject. They analysed the different degrees of territorial identification, the feelings of belonging and identity, from European to local, and compared these with the responses given by older adults: the data can also be compared at the level of the Spanish state. The findings of this survey, with those from Martin Serrano and Velarde (2001) and Orizo and Elzo (2001) provide the basic data for this chapter.

Although there is general agreement that identity is created from the different systems which people feel part of, such as family, job and political opinion, territorial belonging, as Table 1 shows, also constitutes an important reference point for personal identification. The Spanish population have strong links to the local environment, such as the city, county and region, but these links and feelings of belonging decrease with distance: a good example of this is shown in the distant and abstract references to the European Union or to the Latin American cultural area. Young people's feelings of territorial identity are weaker than those of the rest of population, except when the reference is to the world; and they probably tend to be more interested in global media than adults. To a great extent, the global media are the leading edge of globalisation (Jensen Arnett, 2002).

In general, these indicators of territorial belonging are used in surveys to define degrees of *localism* and *cosmopolitanism*, since both can be considered as attitudes towards territorial identification (Martin Serrano and Velarde, 2001; Moral and Mateos, 1999; Orizo and Elzo, 2001). Localism means a strong feeling of belonging to close and concrete spaces; cosmopolitanism is linked to feelings of identity with much larger units, such as the European Union, the Latin American community and the world. Factor analysis of these

Table 1: Degrees of territorial identification, on a scale 0 to 10
(Source: Moral and Mateos, 1999, p 10)

	Young people (15-29)	General population (30+)
Town or city	7.8	8.4
County	7.5	8.4
Autonomous Region	7.5	8.3
European Union	5.6	6.4
Latin America Community	4.5	6.3
The world	6.2	–

items shows that localism could explain 47 per cent of the variability while cosmopolitanism only 24 per cent. However, it is difficult to isolate the independent variables associated with both concepts and as a result it is difficult to identify the profiles of local or cosmopolitan young people. The most significant data is probably the correlation between educational level and cosmopolitanism: university students are more likely to claim a global identity which gives a sense of belonging to a world-wide culture (the European Union, the world). Nevertheless, the differences are not very strong: on a scale from 0 to 10, the cosmopolitan identification average was 5.3 for University students, 4.3 for those with only primary education, 4.8 for those with vocational education, and 5.0 for those with secondary education. Families were also found to have an influence on the level of cosmopolitanism: young people from higher socio-economic status families tended to have more cosmopolitan identities (Martin Serrano and Velarde, 2001).

Since the 1990s a change has been noted in the Spanish population towards localism and this could be considered as a trend in the types of identity people adopt (Elzo, 2002; Orizo and Elzo, 2001). Similar trends among younger generations are shown in table 2. This is not surprising, since the family is a strong element in identity, and their ties are bound to territorial belonging. A similar tendency was observed in analysing results that relate localism with a variable which

Table 2: Young peoples' feeling about their identity (15-29)
(Source: Martín Serrano and Velarde, 2001, p 372)

	1996 (n= 6000)	2000 (n= 6492)
Town/city	41%	51%
County	10%	9%
Autonomous Region	12%	10%
Spain	20%	14%
World	11%	8%
No where, everywhere	3%	5%
Don't know	3%	3%
Total	100%	100%

the authors call 'living at home with pleasure': local identity is dominant among younger adolescents, both boys and girls. As well as the family, schools mediate these influences: students attending private schools show a lower localism, and cosmopolitanism is greater in students at religious private schools, while state schools students show a more local identity. This data supports the hypothesis that a status that is adapted to social change allows alternative identities to localism.

Concerning feelings for territorial belonging, these surveys indicate that an important point of reference is birthplace. The processes of internal Spanish migration have almost ended: consequently most adolescents and young people (88 per cent) live in the region where they were born. In the adult population, only 60 per cent of those in Madrid were born there, 68 per cent in Catalonia and 71 per cent in the Basque Country. Where young people have moved to a different region, they tend to identify themselves with the new region (56 per cent). The younger age group (15 to 19 years) have a stronger identification (71 per cent), with the new place than older young people probably because they moved at an early age; older age groups show a similar level of identification with both places.

Table 3: Youth identity in some Autonomous Regions
(Source: Moral and Mateos, 1999, p 10)

Autonomous Regions	Spanish Identity	Dual Identity Regional/ national	Regional Identity	NS/ NC	Total %
Castille and Leon	42%	52%	4%	2%	100%
Madrid	30%	59%	8%	3%	100%
Valencia	28%	57%	13%	2%	100%
Andalucia	13%	66%	19%	2%	100%
Catalonia	16%	40%	43%	1%	100%
Galicia	6%	48 %	45%	1%	100%
Basque Country	5%	42 %	51%	2%	100%

The existence of a dual identity can be seen in all the surveys analysed: a sense of being Spanish as well as being a member of a region is found in about 55 per cent of young people. In other words, they affirm that part of their identity is rooted in their region, while another part comes from their relation to the common state culture. Around 16 per cent feel exclusively Spanish or a member of only one region, but these general figures cover a wide range of regional and local variations in identity affiliations. The differences between some Spanish regions are shown in table 3.

Table 3 shows how a weaker attachment to state identity is found among those people with the strongest sense of regional belonging: the Basque Country, Galicia, and Catalonia, are clear examples of this. In these territories the feeling of dual identity does not reach 50 per cent, probably because of their stronger cultural features which are due to their language. The Basque Country illustrates the strongest sense of territorial identity, which in another study was as high as 56 per cent (Elzo, 2000). Martin Serrano and Velarde (2001) suggested that the mother tongue could be a relevant item in under-standing the young people's territorial identification: those who identified as having only a Spanish identity came from Spanish speaking families, while those supporting only a regional identity were associated with families that had a different mother tongue. However, it was also observed that in the Basque Country and Galicia regional identity was preferred, even among young Spanish speakers. Castille-Leon (4 per cent) and Madrid (8 per cent) can be placed at the other end of the spectrum, where young people offered regional identity in a very small percentage of cases.

Small differences were found between girls and boys, girls being more likely to associate with dual identity (58 per cent) than with regional identity (22 per cent); amongst the boys, 51 per cent stressed a dual identity and 26 per cent felt a stronger regional sense of belonging. The data also showed that level of study was of little relevance. The analysis of political ideologies showed further correlations: broadly, the young people more to the left had stronger feelings of belonging to the local territory. Young people closer to conservative parties chose only a Spanish identification. Finally, those who selected a dual identity were normally close to centre political opinions.

The development of feelings of identity and belonging during adolescence also needs to be analysed, since this period is considered a critical stage in the development of social identity. In Bilbao, in the Basque Country, Molero (1999) carried out research on this, with a sample of 160 children aged between 6 and 14. Although this was only an initial exploratory study, the results offer interesting points for further discussion. She studied three main aspects: the young peoples' image of the country, their sense of national identity and national symbols. Her results were similar to the studies cited above but she also showed that Basque identity becomes more important than other territorial identities at an early age, 12 to 13 years old. At this age identity is often in a situation of experimental change, and adolescence constitutes a key moment for the development of a stronger regional identity. Adolescents are in the process of transforming their system of self, and perceive themselves as members of a social category with sufficient maturity and autonomy to follow information and experiences beyond the confines of their families (Jensen Arnett, 2002).

The dual linguistic model of education that is developed in the Basque Country also contributes to interesting differences in the construction of identities (Elzo, 2000; Molero, 1999). Those adolescents from families who select schools that have Basque as the principal language of instruction (with Spanish taught as a second language) identify themselves as Basque people. On the other hand, adolescents at schools where courses are mainly in Spanish (with Basque taught as a second language) feel more attached to their Spanish identity. In addition, the selection of national symbols corresponds to this dual situation: generally a minority of Basque young people identified with the Spanish flag (Molero, 1999; Moral and Mateos, 1999). According to Molero, children identifying themselves as Basque have a deeper knowledge about the Basque Country than children with a dual identity (Spanish and Basque). These findings must take into account the role of direct socialisation experiences within restricted reference groups (Lastrucci, 2002).

A view from the difference: the case of Catalonia

Catalonia is an example of a territory where different languages and feelings of belonging coexist. This region has a large industrial tradition and underwent a rapid population growth with the arrival of some half a million people from less developed Spanish regions between 1950 and 1970. These people left their deeply rural areas to settle in an urban industrial society with a different language and culture, and their integration has deeply influenced Catalan society. In the current period, a new and increasing flow of immigrants from different countries is arriving and again modifying the social landscape. Almost 55 per cent of the current population are descended from the internal migratory wave, and the new process of 'melting' might help to redefine territorial identity. At the same time European integration is giving a new dimension of identity and citizenship. All these changes are taking place in a society with a strong personality but with no state competences, and this produces an interesting situation: the need to assume different identities, added to personal feelings of belonging.

Catalan society presents an identity characterised by bilingualism, cultural coexistence and high level of social cohesion. Recent surveys (Castells and Tubella, 2003; Estradé *et al.*, 2002) reveal that 92 per cent of young people can clearly define their identity. According to various samples, from 32 per cent to 43 per cent identify themselves as Catalan, or as more Catalan than Spanish; around 36 per cent identify as both Catalan and Spanish, and less than 20 per cent as mainly Spanish. Those identified as Catalan increase with the age range (46 per cent of 26 to 29 years olds). The level of education also seems to influence the identity selected: young people with higher educational levels and who are aligned to centre-left political opinions show a greater identification with Catalan than occurs among the adult group. In the last ten years, the identity selected has shifted clearly towards a shared identity (Catalan and Spanish), at the expense of the pure Catalan or pure Spanish positions. The group defined as only Spanish is clearly declining. This shared identity is accepted without tensions.

Other surveys (Ferrer, 1999; Orizo and Roque, 2001) also reveal an identity strongly rooted in the territory: 67 per cent of the population under 30 years were born in the area and 87 per cent of them had not moved during the previous five years. Of those who did move, almost 99 per cent moved within Catalonia. This low level of mobility makes the local relationships more strong: more than 70 per cent of the sample meet their parents at least once a week. This data seems to reinforce the fact that the family in Catalan society remains a strong element of identity: family links are well consolidated and constitute a basic social network. Another aspect was the perception of the necessary requirements to be considered as a member of this group (Orizo and Roque, 2001). Of the sample, 61 per cent thought that 'to be born' in the territory was a basic requirement, but this was followed by elements of personal ascription such as 'the willingness to be a Catalan' (45 per cent) or 'to live and work in Catalonia' (52 per cent). As many as 89 per cent of Catalan people said that the conviviality between the two cultures of Spanish and Catalan was very good, which explains the profile of a Catalan identity as going far beyond simple ethnic origins shows a different feeling of belonging.

This trend towards a shared identity can be found in all cultural aspects and language is a clear example. The children of internal immigrants who arrived in the 1960s were taught Catalan in school, so the average level of understanding of the language among young people has increased to 99 per cent, and those with the ability to read and speak to 86 per cent. Nevertheless, the social use of the language is declining in favour of Spanish. A recent study (Giner, 2000) showed that 53 per cent of the population uses mainly Catalan in daily life, 30 per cent mainly Spanish and 16 per cent both languages. Paradoxically there seems to be a strong territorial identification even among the non-Catalan speaking groups. For example, in the metropolitan region of Barcelona, where 60 per cent of the Catalan population live, 65 per cent of the population use Spanish as the most familiar language, and only 33 per cent Catalan, although the percentage of shared and territorial identities is around the average.

In modern times, language has been crucial in the definition of a cultural area. Globalisation is affecting cultures and as a consequence the trend towards shared or multiple identities is being accelerated. In the case of plurinational states, the post modern trend could be that people will be able to feel a strong territorial identification, even when their own language is declining in use.

Final remarks

The panorama that has been sketched out here should make us aware of the great complexity and the multiplicity of factors which affect the development of a regional identity (Ruiz Jiménez, 2003). Two basic identities exist side-by-side in Spanish society (Castells and Tubella, 2003; Estradé et al., 2002; Martin Serrano and Velarde, 2001; Moral and Mateos, 1999; Orizo and Roque, 2001; Orizo and Elzo, 2000). As well as a dual identity which combines attachment to both regional and to Spanish elements there is also a general trend towards territorial identity, which is developing among the whole Spanish population, not just among young people (Orizo and Elzo, 2000). Nevertheless, different trajectories can be observed in different regions. Although it is possible to find similar trends in social and economic aspects in all regions, there are others which differentiate them clearly, the principal of these being the degree of regional identification. This is practically non-existent in Spanish regions such as Castille and Madrid, probably because of their location in the historic centre of the modern Spanish state. Other regions show different degrees of identification. Galicia, the Basque Country, and Catalonia present the strongest examples, including rejection of Spanish identity. In two of these regions, the Basque country and Catalonia, independence parties also exist. The historic tradition and culture of these autonomous regions has been reinforced in recent years by a strong associative civil society and by the educational system.

The coexistence of different identities and cultures in the same territory should not be taken for granted. It is commonly accepted in Europe that the preservation of minorities is of great interest, but the concept of 'minority' is complex (Villanueva, 2004). The Spanish example of regional decentralisation is one way of coping with internal territorial identities, but it leaves many questions unanswered. The situation is different from many other European countries, where different identities coexist: Italy, United Kingdom, France, the Netherlands, Finland, Romania and Slovakia, for example. Though there are aspects in common, there are also differences, regional, numerical and social, that make it difficult to find common and simple policies in Europe. This diversity could be an example of the difficulties in managing the current situation. Diversity is an essential European feature. In future the challenge will still be stronger. We need new and more imaginative ways of managing the multiplicity of territorial identities and multicultural issues in 21st century Europe.

4

Muslim adolescents in Europe

Louise Archer

Popular Representations of Muslim Identities in Europe

Muslim identities are currently highly topical issues of concern and debate across Europe. Recent world events have heightened popular fears of 'fundamentalist' Islam, and Muslim people are currently subjected to widespread racism and xenophobia.

The relative academic silence around Muslim adolescents' identities stands in stark contrast to their high profile within media and social spheres, where Muslim identities are widespread objects of popular concern and fear. Negative stereotypes have been fuelled by numerous high profile events such as the Salman Rushdie affair in early 1990s[1], through to the so-called riots between Asian and white youths in a number of English northern towns in 1995 and 2001. This pattern continues with global fears of fundamentalist terrorism following the events of September 11 2001. Within this climate, young Muslims, particularly young men, have been positioned as dangerous social problems, who are the object of fear and suspicion. In British educational policy, Muslim young people have also been identified as problematic pupils, with low levels of academic achievement and low rates of progression into post-compulsory education. Attention has been drawn to teachers' particularly negative views of Muslim pupils and their families and to the popular assumption that Muslim families are repressive and authoritarian (Ballard, 1994; Verma *et al.*, 1994). Research also indicates that many new teachers in Britain do not feel prepared for teaching in multi-ethnic classrooms (TTA, 2003). Jones (1999) points to widespread racist assumptions among educators.

Across Europe the pathologisation of young Muslim identities has also been played out within the educational sphere, focusing around the issue of whether Muslim schoolgirls should be able to wear the headscarf (*hijab*) or the veil (*dbuttah*) in school. For example, there was widespread coverage of recent events in France when Muslim girls were banned from wearing headscarves in school and in public buildings[2] (Broughton, 2004; Henley, 2003; see also Tutiaux Guillon in this volume). A similar ban operates in Turkey, where the wearing of *hijab* is prohibited in universities and other public/educational buildings. There has also been coverage of cases in Germany, where a Muslim teacher was refused a job because she wore the headscarf, and in Oklahoma in the USA where a sixth grade pupil was suspended for wearing a headscarf to school (Buaras, 2003). In contrast, educational institutions in the UK are encouraged to follow a multi-cultural approach and schools are expected to support religious and ethnic diversity and allow pupils to follow their religious and cultural traditions.

Theories of ethnic and cultural identity development

Different theories have been put forward for understanding identity development among young people from minority ethnic backgrounds. Positivistic social psychological theories (Hutnik, 1991; Phinney, 1990) have suggested that minority ethnic young people are caught between what are termed 'majority' and 'minority' cultures and experience cultural conflict moving between these two worlds. Such approaches treat cultures as unified, discrete and mutually exclusive entities and privilege majority (western, white) culture because 'pro'-majority group identifications (assimilation and acculturation) are assumed to be the most beneficial forms of identification for ensuring 'good' mental health and psychological adjustment (Phinney and Alipuria, 1990).

Positivistic approaches tend to represent minority ethnic cultures as problematic due, for example, to their assumption that Asian and Muslim young people suffer from 'culture conflict' in negotiating the two worlds of home and school (Ghuman, 1994; Hiro, 1991). Asian families have been strongly linked to notions of 'culture', which is represented as authoritarian, sexist, repressive, and 'traditional', as opposed to schools and majority society which is assumed to be modern, secular, liberal and western. As various critics have argued, culture conflict models pathologise Asian families and identities and ignore the existence of racism and other axes of identification (Archer, 2003; Brah, 1992; Dwyer 1999). Positivist approaches are thus questioned for

- treating cultures as static and homongenous

- privileging western cultures and problematising minority cultures

- ignoring racism

- suggesting that ethnic identifications are inherently more problematic for minority ethnic groups than for the white majority.

Rattansi (1992) has questioned the popularly assumed linkage between Asians and Muslims with notions of 'culture'. He explains how key official reports on race/ethnicity and education singled out 'Asian' culture, exemplified as 'the Asian family', to explain the contrast with other communities, although as Rattansi argues, there is no singular form of Asian culture. And yet these racist typologies continue within popular, media and policy discourses. Recently, for example, Muslim communities have been positioned as 'dangerous cultures', whose loyalty to western states cannot be counted upon. Concerns have also been expressed about so-called 'inward-looking' Muslim cultures and 'disaffected' Muslim youth (Lewis, 2001). Indeed, Shain (2003) notes how David Blunkett, the former British Home Secretary, has conjured up images of an isolated Muslim community that 'clings to backward practices, does not bother to learn the English language and does not want to integrate into mainstream society' (p viii).

However, critical literature suggests that young people's identities need to be conceptualised in more complex terms, taking account of cultural aspects of identity development, such as the interplay between race/nationality, religion, ethnicity, gender, class and generational status. 'Race', ethnicity, culture and identity are all socially constructed phenomena: they are not natural, biological or clear-cut entities. Indeed, 'no persuasive empirical case has been made for ascribing common, psychological, intellectual or moral capacities or characteristics to individuals on the basis of skin colour or physiognomy' (Donald and Rattansi, 1992, p 1).

The work of Stuart Hall (1992, 1996) is particularly useful in demonstrating how the meanings of particular ethnic, religious or cultural identities are socially and historically specific and that they are unstable, always in the process of being made, re-made, given meaning and contested. Hall argues that all knowledge is contextual and draws attention to the role of 'history, language and culture in the construction of subjectivity and identity' (Hall, 1992, p 257). Thus the meanings of ethnicity and the boundaries of 'cultures' and identities are permeable and shifting, engaged in a process of constant change (Anthias and Yuval-Davis, 1992). Ethnic and religious identities are also 'culturally entangled' (Hesse, 2000) with other forms of identification. For example, 'ethnicity is often constructed in relation to particular notions of masculinity and femininity and these ideals are used to create, regulate and maintain particular ethnic group identities' (Archer, 2003, p 20). The remainder of this chapter is organised into two sections, examining how Muslim girls and boys construct their identities.

Muslim Girls' Identities

Muslim girls have been stereotypically represented as passive victims of oppressive, patriarchal home cultures. This section compares these 'common sense' views with evidence from Muslim girls' own accounts of their identities and lives. It is argued that far from being passive cultural 'victims' Muslim girls actively construct complex and diverse, multi-layered, femininities.

'We're not like that': rejecting the 'two worlds' discourse

Research shows that young British Muslim women actively challenge dominant representations of themselves and produce new meanings. For example, one of Claire Dwyer's respondents argued that 'people think Muslim women are not allowed to go out, they are not allowed to do this, they have to cover themselves, they're chained to the kitchen sink, but we're not like that' (Dwyer, 1998, p 50). Similarly, Muslim secondary school girls in my own research (Archer, 1998; 2002a; 2002b) emphasised that they had happy home lives in which they enjoyed parental support for a wide range of personal, social and educational choices. The girls also adopted distinctly hybrid, British/English Muslim identities, arguing that they defined themselves both by their nationality/country of birth (English/British) and their religious identity (Muslim). In contrast to the boys, the girls felt that these two identities were inextricably linked (e.g. 'We're English Muslims, that's what we are' (Shireen); 'We're British Muslims' (Nasreen)). Again, these findings challenge the popular assumption that Muslim girls suffer from what is called 'culture conflict' as a result of being caught 'between two worlds'.

Farzana Shain (2003) conducted research with Asian girls in a number of secondary schools and found that they employed a variety of different identity strategies, which she termed 'resistance through culture', 'survival', 'rebellion against culture' and 'religious prioritisation'. Shain found that the most commonly used strategy was 'resistance through culture', which was primarily adopted by 'gang girls' (in Shain's terminology). These girls preferred all-Asian female friendship groups and defined themselves and their experiences through racism, against which they asserted more positive 'Asian' identities. Shain's study revealed how these girls had predominantly poor relationships with their teachers, who viewed one another as 'trouble-makers' and 'racists' respectively. The girls did not expect to continue in education after the age of 16, which, from a popular/ stereotypical viewpoint, might be interpreted as showing that the girls were oppressed by patriarchal home cultures which do not value education for girls. Shain reveals, however, that these girls were active in the production of the expectation that they would not continue into post-compulsory education, through their behaviour and attitudes. Despite their parents' wishes, these girls did not want to continue in education and regularly truanted and treated school first and foremost as a place to have fun and meet friends. Whilst she did find evidence of some girls complaining about sexism in Asian cultures, this was only one response among several (and of course such arguments can be found among many cultures – including diverse white European families!).

In order for educators, researchers and other professionals to engage more equitably and sensitively with Muslim young women, it is useful to interrogate taken-for-granted, 'common sense' understandings of what constitutes 'normal' femininity. Critical researchers have drawn attention to how particular, Eurocentric (and heterosexist) assumptions underpin many dominant ideals about normal adolescent femininity – against which Muslim and other minority ethnic group girls are often judged to be different or abnormal. For example, it is often assumed that normal adolescent girls want to wear western clothes and make-up and partake in particular leisure activities, such as going out, drinking and engaging in heterosexual relationships. However, this is only one version of 'normal' or desirable femininity, to which many girls, including many Muslim girls, do not necessarily subscribe. For example, many of the Muslim girls in my research study had no desire to drink or go to pubs, bars or night-clubs. Their reasons for not wanting to go out and to occupy public spaces, unlike many of their male Muslim peers, were explained as reflecting both a strategy for avoiding racism, a daily experience of the girls' lives, and a positive enjoyment of/preference for private female friendship and family circles.

It is also important to note that young people's identities are not formed in cultural isolation: they are shaped and inflected by the wider context of interpersonal, social and institutional relations. For example, Dwyer (1998, 1999) examined how young Muslim women negotiated their identities in relation to a complex web of ideas and attitudes of teachers and pupils at school, family and home environments and wider societal discourses, such as the media. These discussions often centred around notions of 'appropriate' femininities, which the girls articulated in relation to parental, familial, peer, school and societal expectations. Identities and expectations were framed within a range of conflicting racialised and gendered assumptions about female labour, work/employment, the upholding of collective Muslim 'honour' (*izzat*) and classed school cultures and career expectations. Girls in my own research also engaged in lengthy debates about what it means to be a 'proper' Muslim and what might constitute 'respectable' or appropriate Muslim femininity. None of these meanings were fixed: they were all subject to ongoing debate and challenge.

Like the Muslim girls in Dwyer's research (1998, 1999), the girls in my study also challenged notions of a traditional-western dichotomy through their appearance, dress and styles. They talked about mixing their styles of clothing and appearance to match personal preference and to accord with different contexts. These actions were imbued with a range of different meanings which disrupted any simple equation between clothing and religious, ethnic or national identification.

Wearing hijab: *negotiating meanings*

Educational debates in Europe have focused on the meanings and implications of Muslim girls wearing head scarves (*hijab*) in educational settings. Those wishing to ban the practice have appealed on two main issues: citing concerns about the inappropriate expression of religious identities within secular state education and that the veil represents the oppression of women. Sixty prominent French women signed a petition, published in *Elle* magazine, calling for a ban on 'this visible symbol of the submission of women' (Henley, 2003). In opposition, critics like Bullock (2002, cited in Ahmad, 2003) have argued that the assumption that the *hijab* represents female oppression reflects a colonial feminist construction of Muslim women, which foregrounds dominant 'liberal' notions of equality and privileges western political interests.

Fauzia Ahmad's research (2001) with Muslim South Asian women in higher education reveals that there are many and multiple variations between Muslim women in terms of both the wearing (or not) of the *hijab* and the religious meanings and interpretations that they associate with their actions. Drawing on both research evidence and her own experiences as a Muslim woman, Ahmad illuminates the vastly different practices and forms of belief and non-belief which exist between Muslim women. She draws on Khan's (1998) suggestion for delineating between the terms 'muslim' and 'Muslim' as a way of engaging with this diversity. Ahmad argues that there is currently an over-emphasis upon the head scarf as a symbol of Muslim femininity, particularly given that *hijab*-wearing Muslim women have been increasingly targeted for racist physical and verbal abuse in many western countries, post-11 September 2001 (see Ahmad, 2003).

In my own research with adolescent Muslim pupils in Britain, young women emphasised the contradictions and assumptions surrounding the wearing or not of headscarves by Muslim girls. They engaged in animated discussions about how wearing the scarf did not necessarily denote adherence to strict religious or sexual values or behaviours, and a range of potential counter-interpretations were offered. For example, it was suggested that a girl might wear *hijab* 'for fashion', or to please her parents or as an expression of her faith, and for a combination of reasons across different times and places. Again, the young women's views challenged assumptions of the traditional-western dichotomy and disrupted popular stereotypical readings of Muslim women's wearing of *dbuttah*/*hijab*. As Nasreen, a young Muslim woman explained, 'we don't come to school and put our make-up on and then go home and wear *dbuttah* and stuff like that – it's not like that'.

Muslim Boys' Identities

Over the years, popular representations of Muslim boys have changed considerably. Prior to the current Islamophobia, British Muslim boys were often subsumed within stereotypes of 'Asian' boys. These stereotypes were predominantly framed in passive terms: a number of different studies have detailed how teachers and other pupils view Asian boys as effeminate, 'quiet and little'

(Connolly, 1998), well-behaved and highly achieving pupils (Mac an Ghaill, 1988; Gillborn, 1990). However the Salman Rushdie affair helped to bring differences between Muslims and other Asian pupils to the fore. This was encapsulated in a new popular distinction between Indian (Hindu/Sikh) 'achievers' and Pakistani/Bangladeshi 'believers' (Modood, 1992). Muslim boys are now commonly represented as 'dangerous' and educationally problematic young people. This section compares these common myths to the ways in which Muslim boys have described their identities and lives.

Beyond the stereotypes: gangsters, gangs and fundamentalists

In her book, *The Asian Gang*, Claire Alexander (2000) outlines and discusses some of the most common stereotypical images and representations of Muslim boys in the British media. She cites newspaper reports about teenage gangs of Muslim boys who are supposedly 'terrorising' cities and towns. She demonstrates how images of Muslim youth are used to signify urban decay, poverty, crime and disaffection. In short, she argues, Muslim youth are often represented in social and policy discourse as 'a demographic time bomb' (Alexander, 2000, p 7). They appear to be the new folk devils of the western world, regarded as not just personally, but culturally dangerous. For example, various right-wing political commentators have decried Muslim identities and beliefs as threatening the very fabric of 'the British way of life' (for example, Winston Churchill, MP in 1993). These fears have been amplified by recent debates and moral panics surrounding asylum-seekers, in which the terminology of 'invasion', 'swamping' and 'bogus' applications has been particularly applied to Muslim men, who constitute a large proportion of asylum-seeker and refugee groups in the UK, such as Somalis, Turkish-Kurds and Iraqis (Rutter, 2001). The concerns about young male Muslim identities in Britain are also detailed by Lewis (2001, p 1), who describes the world of 'young Muslims at street level' as characterised by gangs, violence, petty crime and sexism, coined as 'the world of Ali G'[3].

However, critical research has attempted to move beyond these narrow racist stereotypes. Alexander, for example, conducted ethnographic research with young Muslim men in London, observing their identities, behaviours and friendship groups over several years. Her findings revealed that the young men's so-called 'gangs' were highly complex, shifting groups, whose membership changed and evolved across time and context. Furthermore, the 'gang' was not restricted to particular age groups, families, cultures, people or places. As a number of other studies also demonstrate, gangs and other male friendship groupings are often linked to particular places and may revolve more around issues of territoriality, safety and masculinity than crime and disaffection. Furthermore, these issues are not solely the preserve of Muslim boys, but have been noted across a variety of ethnic, national and religious contexts, including white Protestant and Catholic boys in Northern Ireland (Connolly and Neill, 2001), African Caribbean boys (Westwood, 1990) and diverse groups of boys in London (Archer and Yamashita, 2003).

My own research indicates that British Muslim boys draw on and construct a range of ethnic, national, religious and popular masculinities (see Archer, 1998, 2001, 2002a, 2002b, 2003). For example, during discussion groups boys variously aligned themselves as 'Muslim', 'black' and/or 'Asian', as well as trying out aspects of 'gangster' masculine identities. Black identities were utilised within the context of racism and Asian identities were mostly drawn on when discussing gender relations. Boys also aligned themselves with particular national and regional identities, such as Kashmiri, Pakistani and Bangladeshi, when discussing intra-Asian relationships and issues. Across the board, however, boys said that they were proud to identify themselves first and foremost as 'Muslim', claiming this to be the most important identity, over and above their other ethnic, national, cultural and linguistic identities. Yet the boys varied considerably in their differing interpretations of what constitutes 'real' Muslim identity, and debated as to whether they themselves were 'authentic' Muslims. During these negotiations, the boys compared themselves to Muslim girls and to white peers when justifying the authenticity of their own Muslim identities, and to older generations of Muslims (particularly Muslim men and their parents) when suggesting that 'we're not *proper* Muslims'.

A few of the boys expressed what might be considered as extreme views regarding Salman Rushdie, such as suggesting that they would 'chop him up' if he ever came to their town, and some espoused aspects of the 'rude boy' image. However, these views were always expressed within specific contexts and constituted only one subject position/identity among many others. Thus, boys expressed a range of contradictory identities across the discussion groups, shifting between portraying themselves as both 'good' and 'bad', depending upon the subject under discussion. The boys' constructions of 'gangster' and 'hard' Muslim masculinities can be interpreted as part of their wider displays of masculinity. These displays include engaging in verbal jousting and discursive 'jockeying for position' (Edley and Wetherell, 1997) and are often directed more at the audience in question, rather than reflecting a consistent, homogenous world view or behaviour. Instead, the boys took up and tried on a variety of identities within different contexts.

'Talking tough' involved reproducing racialised myths and demonstrating particular knowledge and experiences about gangs, violent/ criminal activities and certain fashions/ styles and it enabled some boys to gain social status, discursive space and masculinity capital in relation to both other boys and the interviewer/researcher. The nature and form of this talk and identification varied between the groups, reflecting interpersonal and contextual differences. For example, only boys who took part in discussion groups with the Asian female interviewer discussed the Salman Rushdie incident. They also used particular forms of sexist talk in order to assert themselves, and their racial 'authenticity', in relation to an interviewer from 'their own' background. It may therefore be useful for educators and researchers to look beyond the surface value of young people's talk in order to examine, and address, the forms of masculinity that lie beneath it.

'Doing Masculinity': Muslim Masculinity as relational

Whilst popular representations portray Muslim masculinity as a discrete (and alien) phenomenon, Alexander (2000) argues that Muslim young men's identities are actually highly relational, formed through multiple frames of reference. Similarly, Shain (2003) draws a link between the increase in popular fears of angry or fundamentalist Muslim masculinity with a corresponding increase in stereotypes of passive, controlled, oppressed Muslim femininity. Across all the discussion groups in my research, it was clear that the boys' talk was simultaneously orientated at both real and imagined audiences across a number of levels. For example, by recounting their knowledge or experience of gangs and criminal activities, boys were able to resist dominant stereotypes that represent Asian boys as passive or effeminate. It also provided a means to challenge experiences of powerlessness engendered by the daily racisms which they encountered both in and out of school. Furthermore, even those boys who adopted the most strident views were still keen to distance themselves from 'really bad' forms of gangster masculinity or religious fundamentalism. They thus negotiated between being 'bad enough' (for example, claiming racialised patriarchal dividends *vis-à-vis* Muslim girls and enjoying respect/fear from other boys) and 'not too bad' (to avoid being revealed as inauthentic and to maintain a general valuing of education, family and religious identification in relation to their families, the school and the researchers).

The topic of sexism has been frequently associated with Muslim boys, although as much feminist research demonstrates, the issue can equally be applied to all boys. However, many white practitioners and researchers have expressed concerns about how to interpret and 'treat' issues of sexism amongst pupils from minority ethnic backgrounds, for fear of being accused of cultural insensitivity. Many of the boys in my study expressed quite sexist and stereotypical views of Muslim girls, but I interpreted these views as forming part of the boys' everyday performances of masculinity. Across the discussion groups, boys constructed their masculine identities by appealing to 'the protection of femininity' (Wetherell, 1993), or more specifically, to the protection of Muslim femininity. For example, boys suggested that it was 'natural' or 'traditional' for them to try to police and surveil the appearance and behaviour of their Muslim female peers, whilst operating a system of double standards in relation to their own dress and actions. The patriarchal benefits of such a situation were clearly acknowledged: as one boy put it, 'it's good for us, innit, we're lads!'. The boys also actively engaged in perpetuating a range of myths about Muslim girls, such as claiming that they are 'not allowed' to continue in education, have no choices in terms of their education or future marriages and are 'forced' to stay at home performing domestic chores for their families.

An uncritical reading of the above examples might take such views as evidence of the oppressive cultures thesis. However, I suggest that they might be seen as revealing the everyday reproduction of racialised masculinities. This view is reinforced when we consider how the boys' accounts were roundly challenged not only by the majority of girls in the study, but by their own admission, when boys recognised the disjuncture between these idealised accounts and their real life experiences of gender relations. Indeed, several boys also complained bitterly that Muslim girls are 'out of [their] control'. The boys' talk can be understood as orientated to multiple audiences: other boys, girls, and the interviewers. It not only functions as 'tough talk', to bolster the speaker's kudos in a particular context, but allows the boys to attempt to establish themselves as spokespersons on Muslim and Asian 'culture'. This, as Anthias and Yuval-Davis (1992) argue, is a powerful symbolic discursive position that addresses a far wider audience. The examples provided can be understood as reflecting the different ways in which different Muslim boys' attempted to perform hegemonic/patriarchal masculinities within particular interview contexts. Whilst the boys' identities may differ in certain ways from other boys' performances of masculinity, it is important to remember that all boys' masculine identities are formed within racialised and classed contexts. Masculine identities are inflected in different ways according to the specific ethnic/racial and classed relations within which they are produced. Hence boys, positioned within structural inequalities such as racism, may assert an additional emotional attachment to certain forms of masculinity that convey power and status and allow them to resist particular dominant stereotypes of themselves and which provide access to power *vis à vis* other social groups.

Conclusion

The aim of this chapter has been to provide the reader with some alternative ways of understanding Muslim adolescents and their identity development. This is clearly an important issue since many majority group researchers, policy makers and practitioners report feeling unprepared to work with minority ethnic groups. The effects of ethnic and racial stereotyping upon minority ethnic young people are well documented and it is crucially important for all professionals to reflect critically upon the concepts, terminology and assumptions they adopt in relation to young people. Thus the conceptual frameworks adopted by educators, researchers and policy makers in their work with young Muslims are crucially important: these views play a role in the shaping of the young people's identities and experiences and have the potential to either help challenge, or create/reinforce, inequalities in their lives.

Muslim identities are complex, diverse and multi-layered, and are formed relationally to other identities and to racism. For example, boys may be active in the reproduction of particular stereotypes of Muslim femininities in order to produce masculine advantages, although these attempts may often be actively resisted by girls. Girls also produce diverse constructions of wearing *hijab* and many actively resist being positioned as 'between two worlds'.

It is also important to emphasise that this chapter does not try to deny that there are instances of oppression, injustice or cause for concern among Muslim families and young people: these will occur in any community. Rather, the aim has been to challenge some of the preconceived, dominant stereotypes and narrow representations of Muslim youth that abound. The goal has been to open up rather than to close down, or simply replace, ways of thinking about Muslim identities. Emphasis has been placed on the interlinking and 'entanglement' of race, ethnicity, religion, nationality and gender in young people's identities to reveal some of the complex ways in which inequality, culture and identity are interlinked.

So the solutions to the problems associated with/experienced by young Muslims will need to address wider contexts within which these young people are situated, particularly issues of racism and poverty. As Shain (2003) argues, a key goal will be to work towards providing safe educational environments for pupils in which pervasive everyday racisms and sexisms are effectively challenged.

Notes

1 The publication of Indian/ British author Salman Rushdie's novel *The Satanic Verses* (1988) sparked widespread protest, as the book was deemed by some commentators to be 'anti-Muslim'. Ayatollah Khomeini (the Iranian religious leader) declared a *fatwah* (death penalty) on Rushdie and numerous protests took place in which copies of the book were publicly burnt.

2 The report recommends banning all conspicuous religious symbols, irrespective of any particular faith, in order to preserve the French secular state.

3 Ali G is the comic creation of the comedian/satirist Sascha Baron Cohen. The character plays up to a 'rude boy' image, espousing drugs, hyper-heterosexuality, rap music, etc.

5

The identities of youths of Chinese origin: the case of the British-Chinese

Becky Francis, London Metropolitan University

Introduction

The experiences and identities of the Chinese, and people of Chinese origin, in Europe, remains a relatively under-researched area. Yet the small body of work analysing Chinese lives in the European context is growing, and interest has begun to turn to the identities of young people from this ethnic group, who are often of second or third generation. The findings of such research will be discussed here. I shall begin by providing a brief history of Chinese migration to Europe generally, and to Britain specifically. The economic and social situation for the Chinese in Britain will be outlined. We shall then turn to British-Chinese youths, examining their educational achievement, and perceptions of British-Chinese youths by others. The following, largest section will attend to British-Chinese constructions of their identities, discussing their construction of ethnic identity, aspirations and outlooks, and the values that they position as 'Chinese'. Their constructions of gender will also be examined. In this way I shall endeavour to provide an overview of evidence concerning construction of British-Chinese youth identities.

Chinese migration to Europe

Well-established Chinese communities can be found across the globe – many communities in different parts of South-East Asia are particularly large and longstanding. Yet from the second half of the 20th century to the present day, the majority of migrants from China and Hong Kong have travelled to the West (Gungwu, 1998). For Hong Kong Chinese, who comprise the majority of the Chinese community in Britain, Britain, Canada, and Australia have in recent years been popular destinations, but as Gungwu observes, the Chinese continue to found a living in a diverse range of countries, including many European countries apart from Britain. Pieke (1998) estimates that there are well over half a million Chinese living in Europe. There is higher numeric representation of Chinese in Western European countries than in Eastern Europe, but this may begin to change as the recent expansion in European Union membership ensures that Europe opens up.

The Chinese presence in Europe dates back to the eighteenth century, when Chinese merchant seamen began to settle in port areas (Pieke, 1998, notes communities in London, Liverpool, Rotterdam, Amsterdam, Hamburg, Antwerp and Barcelona). As Baxter and Raw (1988) observe, the need to service off-duty seamen passing between British ports led to the development of small Chinatowns in many British coastal cities, from which former Chinese seafarers were able to sustain a living[1]. Chinese soldiers were also represented in the many European wars in the early 20th century. Pieke (1998) records well over 100,000 Chinese labourers having been recruited by the Allied Forces during the First World War, and Chinese volunteers aiding the Bolsheviks in Russia and the International Brigades in the fight against Franco in Spain. There are political as well as economic factors which explain many of the patterns and directions in Chinese migration to Europe. Examples include the influx of Chinese from Indochina to France following the overthrow of the US-backed regimes in Vietnam, Cambodia and Laos, or the arrival of Indonesian Chinese in the Netherlands following Indonesian independence and the ensuing pogroms against the Chinese. The Chinese in Europe now represent a host of diversities in terms of their place of origin, education level, and social class and/or level of affluence. However, Chinese migration to and living in Europe has been highly circumscribed by the waves of immigration legislation throughout the last century which have variously limited their movements and freedoms (Pieke, 1998, Baxter and Raw, 1988).

Of all the European nations Britain has the largest Chinese population, mainly due to its colonisation of Hong Kong Island and the New Territories in the 19th century. In Britain the catering trade was established as the primary industry among the Chinese: the taste for Chinese food among indigenous populations has rapidly spread to many other European nations. The majority of Chinese and British-Chinese living in Britain today are from families which arrived in the late 1950s and 1960s. This was a period in which village agriculture in the New Territories faced disruption due to a host of political and economic factors and when Britain was appealing to migrant labourers as a consequence of the post-war boom. British people were acquiring a taste for foreign food, and for the convenience and luxury of ready-prepared meals. As in the case of South Asian migrants, Chinese chefs soon learnt to adapt traditional food to cater for local tastes. Hence Chinese food swiftly became popular among the British population.

This pull of demand, coupled with the institutional racism which migrants met when attempting to enter other fields of work, meant that catering became the destiny of the overwhelming majority of Chinese migrants to Britain. As Watson (1977) observed, the lineage system on which Hong Kong social networks were based extended to Britain, with established restaurant workers aiding passage and settlement of new migrants, and often employing them too. Pieke (1998) positions such practices as the inevitable consequences of the Chinese chain migration approach, whereas Baxter and Raw (1988) see it as the consequence of pernicious legislation. They discuss how the 1962 Commonwealth Immigrants Act channelled incoming migrants into the ethnic fast-food industry by issuing permits almost exclusively in the catering field. The Act also discriminated against women, as men were allowed to bring spouses and dependants, but women were not. Hence the majority of women were dependants. As dependants were obliged to demonstrate that they could be supported by their sponsors, they were automatically placed in a highly dependent/subordinate position[2].

The Chinese in Britain

So the vast majority of Chinese in Britain are currently concentrated in the catering sector, although evidence suggests that this picture is beginning to change. A Home Affairs Committee Report to the House of Commons (1985) puts 90 per cent of Chinese in Britain as working in catering or related fields, where more recent commentators such as Owen (1994), Parker (1998) and Francis and Archer (2004) found slightly fewer. Chinese restaurants and takeaways are represented right across Britain, with even the most obscure and far-flung outposts often having a local Chinese takeaway. These outlets have made many Chinese in Britain wealthy. Many have come from impoverished lives in the rural New Territories, and have worked their way up through employment in catering to business ownership and become affluent in the process. As my work with Louise Archer discusses (Francis and Archer, 2004, Archer and Francis, forthcoming a and b), through such entrepreneurship, and through the success of their offspring in the British education system, such families are succeeding in swift upward mobility in terms of social class, and transcend and challenge traditional conceptions and categorisations of class.

However, it is vital to bear in mind the hardships, impediments and costs which such individuals have had to bear in order to achieve such success. Work in the catering industry is notoriously hard, with long hours and hard physical work often involved. As Baxter and Raw (1988) and Parker (1998; 2000) attest, many recent immigrants have to endure extremely difficult work conditions, and sometimes women working in family takeaways are have no formal salary at all except what their husband chooses to give them. Parker and Baxter and Raw also catalogue the racist and sexist abuse and harassment which counter staff in takeaways often suffer from the indigenous population. So when reflecting on Chinese success stories, Wong

(1994) and Parker (2000) remind us of the high costs in hardships and deprivations endured by the first-generation Chinese community in order to break the cycle of necessity and to make possible the luxury of choice for their children. This is particularly important given that there is a tendency to stereotype the Chinese in particular ways. They are seen as 'naturally' or 'culturally' industrious, collectivist, deferent, conformist, wedded to Confucian values, and as an 'economic success story' (Wong, 1994; Tam, 1998; Chau and Yu, 2001). These ideas are derived from often racist stereotypes which see the Chinese (like others from the Asian continent) as 'culture rich', but as repressed, oppressing, and problematic (Tam, 1998; Archer, 2003). Moreover, the notion of the Chinese as an economic 'success story' in Britain has meant that they are often seen as not needing help, and as not having difficulties, and consequently tend to be bypassed by social services (Parker, 2000; Chau and Yu, 2001).

Seeking to avoid such stereotypical and essentialising approaches, a number of researchers of the Chinese diaspora have explored the experiences of the Chinese in Britain in terms of Bourdieu's concepts of 'habitus' and 'cultural capital' (for example, Wong, 1994; Parker, 2000; Chau and Yu, 2001). Parker has shown how diasporic habitus has manufactured a sense of 'being Chinese' as a result of displacement, rather than as a result of Confucian values. The social constructionist view of ethnic identity as constructed and relational (Hall, 1993; Ang, 2001) is applied in my analysis of work around British-Chinese youth identities. I also draw on Foucauldian tools of discourse analysis (Foucault, 1980; Burman and Parker, 1993) in order to interrogate the various discourses of race and gender that position people in relations of power.

Perceptions of British-Chinese youth

Scant research has documented the pastimes and preoccupations of British-Chinese youth. Many young British-Chinese are involved to some extent in helping out in their family's takeaways or restaurants (Song, 1997; Sham and Woodrow, 1998; Parker, 2000). This is of course a learning experience and often contributes to family solidarity, being happily accepted by offspring (Song, 1997). At other times such duties may cause resentment, either on the part of young people who feel pressured to participate, or on the part of parents and fellow siblings when young people refuse to participate (Song, 1997). There are also costs in terms of the time spent on such work which could be spent on homework and/or socialising (Sham and Woodrow, 1998). However, increasingly young British-Chinese in more affluent families are protected from such work, with parents keen to ensure that their offspring are spared the hardships which they endured in building a life in Britain (Francis and Archer, 2004).

In terms of the leisure activities of young British-Chinese, Parker (1998) records how there is still much orientation towards Hong Kong culture even among the second and third-generation born in Britain. Many young British-Chinese avidly follow Hong Kong movies and pop songs. Parker (1998) maintains that 'Unlike black and South Asian music and film-making, Hong Kong popular culture has not been further translated into a British idiom' (p 99). This said, Hong Kong's violent martial arts and Triad gangster movies have appealed to and been avidly followed by a minority of non-Chinese British enthusiasts for decades, and such genres have recently become mainstream in the West with the contributions of directors such as John Woo and Ang Lee. The continued engagement of many young British-Chinese with Hong Kong popular culture is of course enabled by the perpetuation of the Chinese language among British-Chinese: parents take this extremely seriously, with a high proportion of young Chinese in urban areas expected to attend Chinese school at the weekend to learn Cantonese (Parker, 1998; Christiansen, 1998; Francis and Archer, 2004). Otherwise, many of their other interests seem to reflect those of their white British counterparts. Commitment to family is constructed as a key aspect of 'Chineseness' by the Chinese, and as highly important (Pang, 1999; Song, 1997; Francis and Archer, 2004). Hence children are often expected to spend a great deal of time with the family. However, suggestions that this precludes social activities with other young people (Woodrow and Sham, 2001) ignore the point that British-Chinese extended families are often large and include a network of young people – cousins, second cousins and so on – who are friends as well as often only slightly related. Hence family time can simultaneously be a time for socialising with other young people.

As a group, British-Chinese pupils are high achievers within the British education system. British-Chinese and Indian pupils out-perform children from other ethnic groups in British compulsory education (DfEE, 2001). Further, over 90 per cent of British-Chinese students continue into full-time post-compulsory education (Owen, 1994) and they are more likely than any other ethnic group in Britain to enter higher education (Gillborn and Gipps, 1996). Writing only two decades ago Taylor (1987) found that relatively few people of Chinese origin entered British higher education: this rapid change illustrates the swift progression of British-born Chinese pupils in terms of educational achievement. Moreover, while concerns about 'boys' underachievement' remain an ongoing theme in the academic and popular press (Epstein *et al.*, 1998; Francis, 2000), figures show that British-Chinese boys, as well as Indian boys, continue to match the educational performance of their female counterparts (Gillborn and Gipps, 1996)[3]. Yet this educational success has rarely been ack-nowledged or analysed by British educationalists. Sham and Wood-row's studies (1998; Woodrow and Sham, 2001) are some of the few to have examined attitudes to education among British-Chinese pupils, asked pupils about their preferred learning styles and percep-tions of the educational environment. Their findings suggest that these pupils may adopt different learning styles from their white British counterparts. They suggest that British-Chinese pupils are conformist, deferent, and that these characteristics may impede their growth and development, although little evidence is presented to justify such claims. In their discussion of Chinese pupils' in the British education system Woodrow and Sham (2001) barely acknow-ledge the high achievement of British-Chinese pupils. Verma *et al.* (1994) have shown how the dominance of the 'compensatory' pers-pective in education (Siraj-Blatchford, 1993) has resulted in ethnic minority groups being viewed in deficit terms, irrespective of their performance.

British-Chinese constructions of identity

In spite of their educational success, the Chinese experience of British education and young British-Chinese people's opinions and identities have rarely been examined. Parker (1998; 2000) and Song (1997) have made vital contributions in this area, which are currently being built on by other studies, answering Parker's call for more analysis of narratives contributing to British-Chinese identities. My research with Louise Archer seeks to explore British-Chinese secondary school pupils' constructions of their ethnic and gender identities, along with their perceptions of education and attitudes to learning[4]. This section begins by exploring what has been said about specific British-Chinese constructions of identity. It goes on to discuss young people's ideas and talk, and the discourses evident in this, to analyse specific aspects of British-Chinese young peoples' constructions of identity.

Writing in the 1970s, Watson (1977) claimed that the Chinese in Britain had resisted the development of a 'British-Chinese' identity. As he was largely researching first-generation migrants, he acknowledged that such identities might be formed by the next generation. However, in a more recent study Parker (1998) explained that he felt from his research data that 'young Chinese people in Britain did not have a very clear sense of identity, that certain stories had not been spoken, and that they had not met fully the narratives of either British or Chinese culture' (p 93). This is interesting because it often seemed that many respondents in my study with Archer had an assured view of their place in the world. Possibly it depends on the definition of 'identity'. Parker (1998) appears to be considering identity as political, involving a politicised conception of ethnic categorisation. He points out that there is less writing and evidence of political action/identification by British-Chinese youth around issues of racism and/or ethnic identity than for black and South Asian youth. Parker observes (2002) that British-born Chinese often perceive themselves as different from their Hong-Kong Chinese contemporaries, being English-speaking, often bilingual, and having undergone a blurring of cultural experiences, as well as of boundaries between leisure, work and school time.

Chan's (2000) work confirms that young British-Chinese have high self-esteem compared to their white-British and Hong Kong Chinese contemporaries, though he notes that boys in all these groups had higher self-esteem than girls did. He argues that despite the social disadvantages they may face, young British-Chinese people have positive feelings about themselves and as members of society. Chan also saya that they gain more self-esteem from school than do their white and Hong Kong Chinese peers.

This finding that young British-Chinese men and women have higher self-esteem than do Hong Kong youths questions views of the Chinese as basically unchanged by their British location. Woodrow and Sham (2001) argue that there is little adaptation into British-European culture even in second and third generation immigrants. They maintain of British-Chinese youths,

> because the cultural impositions are so strong they do not have room for much questioning and this breeds conforming satisfaction of a kind often found in strong religious faiths which leads to little impetus for growth and change. (Woodrow and Sham, 2001)

Besides rejecting the problematising approach implied by the term 'little impetus for growth and change', my findings with Archer contest these arguments. We found a great deal of ethnic mixing in friendship groups, and that British-Chinese shared interests and concerns with, but also distinguished themselves from, youths from other ethnic groups (Francis and Archer, forthcoming). Moreover, our findings show that British-Chinese pupils were very ready to question and challenge both their parents, and the apparent attitudes of their white peers and their parents (see Francis and Archer, 2004; forthcoming; Archer and Francis, forthcoming a).

Findings from my work with Archer demonstrate that local geographies have a strong influence on the construction of identity among pupils from all ethnicities. Particularly for boys, 'race' and social class impacted on conceptions of 'territory' and the policing of such territories. Indeed, ethnicity is clearly bound up with the construction of gender (Mirza, 1992). We found that British-Chinese girls tend to be overwhelmingly constructed by their teachers as obedient and quiet 'good pupils', and de-sexualised. Boys were often constructed in similar ways but teachers' perceptions of a minority of 'bad' British-Chinese led to the construction of a dichotomy where a majority of British-Chinese boys are 'good', but a handful are demonised as 'really bad'. These 'really bad' Chinese boys were often associated with triadism, or seen as having been 'infected' with bad behaviour by white and black working class boys (Archer and Francis, forthcoming b).

Construction of ethnic identity

Examining British-Chinese constructions of ethnic identity, Parker (1998) identifies various constructions of British Chineseness among his young respondents, which he categorises as 'Basically British'; 'Self-regionalisation'; 'Best of Both Worlds'; 'Strong Chinese Identity'; 'Mixed Feelings and Ambivalent Identities'; and 'Multiple and Multifaceted Identity Formations'. A typologies approach to identity risks over-simplification and reductionism (Francis, 2000). Identity is not fixed, but is shifting, contradictory and nuanced (Davies, 1989; Whitehead 2002). As such, typologies can mask such contradictions and nuances, and over-emphasise difference, as there is often extensive overlap in the way different 'groups' respond. On the other hand, if simply presented as illustrative snapshots rather than actual groups, a typologies approach can provide a useful exemplar, as in Parker's (1998) account of British-Chinese ethnic identities. Hampered by lack of space in his chapter, Parker provides relatively little evidence to support some of his types, and it is therefore difficult to ascertain how representative they are, although many seem convincing. As the work of Song (1997) and my study with Archer demonstrate, such British-Chinese constructions of identity are produced in relation to non-British-Chinese 'others'. It would be more useful and flexible to see the various types identified by Parker as narratives supporting and produced by discourses of race, nation and identity, rather than as fixed positions.

Aspirations

In terms of their views and desires concerning their own futures, British-Chinese youths tend to aspire to different work roles than those undertaken by their parents. Pang (1999) found that over half her sample of British-Chinese young people aspired to professional occupations: this is supported by my study with Archer (Francis and Archer, 2004). Our study shows that parents of British-Chinese pupils support these aims: the majority hoped that their offspring would achieve professional careers and explicitly rejected their own catering work as suitable for their children. PuiKeung (parent) says of catering, 'It's a tough occupation isn't it? You work unsociable hours, long hours, you don't have a social life'. They sought to protect their children from the harsh world and work of the catering industry. As Shun Hei (parent) observes, 'I'm working in the kitchen; do I expect my son to work in the kitchen? Of course not. No parent would want their child to do this job. Obviously unless that was the last resort' (Francis and Archer, 2004). Shun Hei's statement turns out to be highly evocative: Pang (1999) found that none of her young British-Chinese respondents wanted to take up catering but many did not rule it out 'as a last resort'. Pang (1999) notes that there is a stereotypical view that the Chinese in Britain aim for the professions, and that her findings confirm this to be the case. However, where white British tend to see such aspirations among the Chinese as solely concerned with status, such desires are actually informed by the wish to avoid the experiences of parents in catering (Francis and Archer, 2004; Pang, 1999). Academic and professional qualifications and professional jobs secure a more comfortable work environment. Pang's longitudinal data shows that two-thirds of those respondents in her sample who aspired to professional jobs went on to achieve their professional status: she maintains that this finding demonstrates that their aims are not unrealistically high, as has been argued by commentators on other ethnic minority groups.

Pang (1999) notes that Chinese adults are more than 3.5 times more likely to enter professional jobs than are whites in Britain, and four times more likely to enter the service sector due to their common work in catering. She maintains that the high number of her respondents who said they might consider catering 'as a last resort', or if they owned their own business, demonstrates that there are still strong ties to catering for the British-Chinese. Indeed, over half her respondents had had experience working in catering, usually in family businesses. So catering offers a safety-net. And although young British-Chinese do not wish to work in catering, Pang found that many of them nonetheless end up doing so.

Pang reports how many in her study believed there is racial discrimination in the British workplace (see also Parker, 1998). Analysing the career choices and pursuits among young British-Chinese, she argues that a strategy is in operation to combat the real or perceived structural constraints of racism in the British labour market. Those British-Chinese who attain good academic qualifications enter the labour market only at the higher levels, whilst the less-qualified Chinese tend to opt for the relative safety of the catering trade. Thus, Pang argues, British-Chinese enter the British workplace only at those levels which minimise the influence of discrimination. Presumably she means discrimination in relation to employment and career, as research has documented how workers in catering outlets are often subject to high levels of racist abuse (for example Parker, 2000).

Pang acknowledges that this apparent tactic among the British-Chinese may not always be successful in avoiding racial discrimination, noting evidence that graduates from minority groups earn less than their white peers, and that this pay differential increases amongst highly qualified workers. She argues that young British-Chinese have adopted a strategy of pursuing vocational subjects such as science, engineering and business, which give them as much leverage as possible in the British market place, and the chance to compete equally, or near equally, with white people. Pang discusses how this approach is gendered, with more British-Chinese women concentrated in health, social and business studies, and applied science. Discussing the extent of concerns about racism in the British labour market among British-Chinese, Pang voices a concern that the focus on Chinese 'success' may conceal the difficulties young Chinese have to overcome in order to achieve.

Construction of Chineseness

In investigating the constructions of identity among British-Chinese pupils, Archer and I have attempted to attend to the specificity of British-Chinese constructions, as distinct from a notion of 'the Chinese' as a homogeneous group (Parker, 1998; 2000; Song 1997). However, many of the British-Chinese pupil and parent respondents to our study are clearly implicated in constructing a notion of 'Chineseness'. Foucault (1978) discusses how we employ 'technologies of the self' to construct ourselves as 'authentic', rational and agentic. In this sense, the construction of identity is an on-going project on the part of individuals. Arguably this notion may be broadened beyond individuals to ethnic groups: the appropriation of particular traits and tendencies as 'Chinese', and the rejection of other characteristics sometimes applied to the Chinese by Westerners, is part of a discursive project to create 'the Chinese community'. So far Archer and I have found two discourses to emerge particularly frequently in British-Chinese pupils' talk about their experiences of the British education system: those of the Chinese 'good pupil', and the 'Chinese value of education' (Francis and Archer, 2004; forthcoming; Archer and Francis forthcoming b). These two discourses were used by the British-Chinese respondents to fashion a positive and proud notion of 'Chineseness': this construction is specific to the British context.

Of course, as with the notion of 'Chineseness' itself, the positioning of Chinese as 'good pupils' and as 'valuing education' can only be conceived in relation to 'others' who do not value education, and who are not good pupils. One of our female respondents explains that Chinese parents believe 'oh, you get a good education and achieve more in life', and so 'probably encourage them [children] more'. Asked whether British-Chinese boys muck about, she replies, 'They can be influenced by other people as well, so'. Hence she positions Chinese families as encouraging their offspring more than other sorts of family do, and suggests that Chinese boys can fall under the influence of such 'others'. 'Other' (non-Chinese) pupils are positioned as a distraction. This supports findings by Song (1997) that British-Chinese families tend to see bad behaviour in

83

their children as being due to what they see as corrupting Western influences.

These themes were echoed in the talk of many of her British-Chinese fellows. Non-Chinese families, and English families in particular, were constructed by British-Chinese pupils as less disciplined and less concerned about their children's education than Chinese families. As noted elsewhere (Francis and Archer, forthcoming), many British-Chinese pupils and many of their teachers constructed Chinese pupils as 'good', but in danger of contamination by the bad behaviour of 'other' pupils. Hence Kitty, a pupil, argues that British-Chinese boys are usually better behaved than others at school because 'the family just wants them to grow a bit harder and achieve the best'. She observes that 'English families are, like, not as strict. And they just you know grow freely'. Archer (2003) discusses a similar construction of white British families as frivolous and irresponsible among South Asian Muslim youths. Kitty later suggests that 'other' boys' bad behaviour might be because 'the family doesn't care about them much or something', illustrating how British-Chinese pupils often constructed white families' apparent lack of concern for their children's education as resulting from a general lack of care (Francis and Archer forthcoming a). This positioning radically contests the Western discourse of 'oppressive home culture' often articulated by white educationalists in concerns about the 'pressure' exerted by Asian parents on their offspring regarding their educational performance (see Francis and Archer, 2004).

There is some evidence that this notion of the Chinese value of education was idealised and not always borne out in practice. For example, Francis and Archer (forthcoming) report how Phil, a pupil, draws on the discourse of a 'Chinese value of education' to maintain that British-Chinese boys tend take their education more seriously than other boys. However, later in his interview when talking about some of his British-Chinese peers, Phil says,

P: Because from my experience I've known quite a lot of people who like, they don't give you know, two fingers about school really. And they go out, they have fun, you know. They join this, they join that [...]

I: So when you're saying they join this, they join that, are you talking about gangs?

P: Gangs and everything, yeah. Because I've known a few. So.

Hence Phil's earlier reification of 'Chinese value of education' contrasts with his discussion of his lived localised experiences which involve gangs and truancy.

The 'Chinese value of education' is a racialised narrative, used by the white population to position the Chinese in a particular way, and it is part of a wider, pernicious discourse that positions the Chinese as diligent, conformist, and self-repressed (Francis and Archer, 2004). Yet it is being used actively by the Chinese in Britain to construct a positive sense of identity. As such, this construction is to some extent a product of diasporic habitus (Bourdieu, 1990; Parker, 2001; Francis and Archer, 2004). Valuing education is reported to be strong among Hong Kong and mainland Chinese, so is far from unique to the Chinese community in Britain. However, it is being drawn on by the Chinese in Britain in particular ways in relation to 'Others' apparent lack of value of education, to construct a positive, proud cultural boundary in the British context (Francis and Archer 2004).

Construction of gender

Archer (2003) has commented that although constructions of gender differ between ethnic groups, the construction of gender as a central and relational aspect of identity remains relatively consistent. Much research has documented how various themes around education are drawn on by boys and girls from different ethnic groups to construct their masculinity and femininity (Reay, 2001; Mirza, 1992; Sewell, 1997; Connolly, 1998; Nayak, 2001; Archer, 2003). The construction of gender among young people of British-Chinese origin is a completely unresearched area. Yet there are suggestions in the initial analyses of the data from my study with Archer that the discourse of the Chinese 'good pupil' and the 'Chinese value of education' may have implications for pupils' positioning in gender discourse.

British-Chinese girls, although articulate and often assertive in their interview responses, were overwhelmingly constructed by their teachers as quiet and obedient 'good pupils', and as a homogenous mass (Archer and Francis, forthcoming b). Moreover, they tended to be de-sexualised, leading us to argue that while girls from other minority ethnic groups are positioned by educationalists as 'oppressed by their home culture', British-Chinese girls are positioned as repressed by their home culture (Archer and Francis, forthcoming a and b). Various researchers have found that South Asian boys are often constructed as effeminate by white and African-Caribbean boys (Mac an Ghaill, 1994; Connolly, 1998). British-Chinese boys, like Indian boys, are a group of 'achievers', and there are indications that their teachers position them in similar ways as not 'real boys'. Conversely, it may be that the popular association of Chinese masculinity with Triad gangsterism and martial arts, which are reflected by the media and entertainment industry, may function as masculine currency for some Chinese boys among their peers. Moreover, there are indications in our data that the elevation of the importance of education among British-Chinese youths means that at least within this ethnic group, boys' educational achievement does not compromise their masculinity. These hypotheses will be explored further as we progress with the data analysis.

Conclusions

As well as providing contextual information about the Chinese in Britain, this chapter has attempted to trace some of diverse ways in which young British-Chinese people construct their identities, and the factors which impact on these constructions. I have shown how particular discourses are drawn on and developed by ethnic groups in their construction of an 'authentic' ethnic community of Chineseness, and how these constructions are specific to the socio-economic environment.

Notes

1 See Baxter and Raw (1988) for an account of the hostility that such settlers faced from indigenous workers and from racist legislature. Chinese seamen were often recruited by European shipping companies to break the power of European sailor unions – Baxter and Raw (1988) and Watson (1977) discuss the case in the British context, while discussion from a pan-European perspective can be found in Pieke, 1998).

2 See Baxter and Raw (1988), Watson (1977); and Parker (1998) for a developed account of the explosion of Chinese catering in Britain, and the structural factors impacting on this. See Watson (1977) for a description and explanation of migration patterns from Hong Kong to Britain.

3 In documenting the high achievement of the British-Chinese as a group, we do not wish to infer that all British-Chinese pupils are high-achieving, or to obscure the problems that British-Chinese pupils face within the British education system, irrespective of their achievement. A focus on the relatively high educational achievement of certain ethnic groups often obscures very high and very low attainment within the same 'group' according to different variables (Gillborn and Gipps, 1996). Moreover, despite their educational achievement, British-Chinese often do not fare so well in employment as similarly qualified white people (Parker, 1998; Pang, 1999).

4 The project is funded by the UK Economic and Social Research Council (ESRC) (Project no. R000239585). It is titled 'British-Chinese Pupils' Constructions of Education, Gender, and Post-16 Pathways'.

6

Ethnic stereotypes and prejudice among Spanish adolescents

Alejandra Navarro and Ileana Enesco

The study of the formation and development of social ideas has become the focus of many developmental researchers, who are aware of how difficult it is to understand adults' ideas and attitudes not knowing how they have been formed. We now have many empirical studies that help us understand how ideas, beliefs and attitudes about social difference are formed in the early years, for example between other races, ethnic groups, languages and religions.

This chapter analyses the problems of prejudice and ethnic-racial attitudes from a developmental perspective. After defining the concepts of prejudice and stereotype, we briefly review different theories about prejudice employed through the 20th century. We then describe the most relevant research findings on the development of ethnic-racial prejudice during childhood and adolescence, with a particular emphasis on studies in Spain.

Prejudices and Stereotypes

Stereotypes can be understood as 'shared beliefs about personal characteristics or personality traits, and very often about specific behaviours, of a group of people' (Leyens, Yzerbyt and Schadron, 1994, p 11). The crucial point in the process of stereotyping a person is to be able to perceive this other person as an exchangeable individual. The stereotype constitutes an extremely simplified and generalised version of what a social group shares when compared to other groups. It comprises not only descriptive elements but also evaluative judgements. Its domain of application is often unlimited. It is possible to hold gender, national or ethnic stereotypes, as well as those related to other social subgroups, such as members of a profession, or those engaged in particular leisure activities. This differentiation can become increasingly specific, beyond any objective limits, because stereotypes are the result of an attribution of differences, not their mere perception. To summarise, the stereotype is not the acknowledgement per se of difference, but the generalisation of certain traits to all members of the group, and the attributions that are made about differences, or the explanations of such traits, which implies evaluation (Augoustinos and Walker, 1995, p 226).

For decades stereotypes were seen as the result of a distorting process in which errors in perception had little or no foundation on reality. Allport (1954) described them as exaggerated, rigid, oversimplified, and incorrect beliefs, equivalent to prejudice. However, more recently writers have tended to distinguish between stereotype and prejudice. Stereotypes are regarded as maps that simplify reality. They help interpret reality, so one can move through it in a fast and usually adequate way. However, they can sometimes lead us to mistakes. The term prejudice is usually reserved for negative and discriminatory predispositions and to derogative judgments about other groups. What these two concepts have in common is that both are overgeneralisations that contain descriptions and explanations that are not neutral: they imply some kind of evaluation.

The boundaries between the two concepts are not very clear and some writers continue to use them as alternatives. However, in this chapter we will define ethnic-racial prejudice as the individual's tendency to perceive, feel, believe, and act towards other ethnic groups in an unfavourable manner. Unfavourable attitudes can range from lack of esteem to hatred, and behaviour can range from avoidance to social rejection and violence (Aboud, 1988; Augoustinos and Walker, 1995).

Theories of prejudice: an historical overview

Explanations for the origins of prejudice have varied over the 20th century. Until approximately 1920, the conception of an unfavourable attitude towards other ethnic-racial groups as 'prejudice' did not exist. As Duckitt (2001) points out, racial dominance, discrimination and generally negative attitudes towards other groups were considered natural responses from 'civilised' people to cope with the 'deficiencies' of 'inferior people', or racially different minorities. The idea of racial superiority was first challenged by scientists after World War I.

Since then social scientists have offered diverse explanations about prejudice, based on different theoretical perspectives. For example, psychoanalytic theorists during the 1930s explained prejudice as an irrational and unconscious process by which a child or an adult conveyed their frustration towards those perceived as different from the dominant majority to those occupying a subordinate position.

As behavioural theories became increasingly influential in psychology, the idea that children lacked prejudices until they learned about them grew at both popular and scientific levels. According to this theory, children learn to evaluate other groups by imitating the attitudes and behaviours that they observe in parents and other significant figures. This was consistent with the idea that prejudice was a social reflection of the prevalent values of a society. Nonetheless, the conceptualisation of prejudice shifted after World War II when social scientists were unable to explain the atrocities perpetrated by the Nazis with the older theories. Adorno's theory was developed in this period: prejudice, intolerance and racism were reinterpreted as the expression of the pathological needs of individuals who had an extreme authoritarian personality.

From the 1980s cognitive approaches suggested new perspectives on prejudice, emphasising the role of normal and universal perceptual-cognitive processes, which were underlying social categorisation. The basic thesis was that the individual's psychological system is prepared to categorise objects, people and events. This process leads to inter-group distinctions, biases, and stereotypes. Taking a developmental perspective based on Piagetian theory, Aboud (1988) adopted a socio-cognitive approach that shows the mutual contributions of these universal cognitive processes and the social experience of the child. From this stance, prejudice is neither a mere social reflex, nor is learned through direct transmission. If this were true, as children grow older they would be more biased, because they would have been more exposed to social stereotypes and prejudices. Prejudices emerge with relative independence from particular experiences, and their development during the later years of adolescence is still a matter of debate between psychologists.

The socio-cognitive approach has been criticised by theorists from the social identity perspective (Tajfel and Turner, 1979) and the self-categorisation theory perspective (Turner, 1987). For example, the research of social psychologists such as Nesdale (2001), Nesdale and Fresser (2001), Rutland (1999) and Verkuyten (2001, 2002) include a greater consideration of the inter-group/societal forces relevant to prejudice, and give more attention to affective factors linked to the social differentiation process.

General trends in the development of ethnic-racial attitudes

Research about the development of attitudes towards different groups dates back to the early developmental studies conducted in the United States with African-American and European-American children. The work of Clark and Clark (1947) had a great impact in the scientific community, reporting deep differences in the development of ethnic identity between white and black children. White children were found to adopt a positive attitude towards their own group and tended to identify with the in-group before they were five years old. In contrast, black children showed lower self-esteem, as shown by their preference for white-skinned images, difficulties *vis à vis* racial identification, and their tendency to undervalue black figures.

Since the 1960s, developmental research into ethnic-racial awareness (Aboud and Amato, 2002) was extended in a number of other multi-ethnic countries (Canada, United Kingdom, Australia, Taiwan, South Africa). In general, those studies reported that children younger than 4 years old displayed a diffuse and not yet biased ethnic orientation. A significant increase in ethnic awareness was noted between the ages of 4 and 7 for white majority group children. At these ages they showed favouritism towards their own ethnic group and negative views towards out-groups.

How prejudice develops during adolescence remains a matter of some debate between researchers. In general, studies prior to the 1970s found that prejudice continues to rise gradually between childhood and adolescence. In contrast, later studies, particularly those conducted over the past two decades, usually report a reduction in ethnic prejudice as adolescence approaches. These differences have been accounted for by the historic changes that took place in US society during the 1960s, following severe inter-ethnic conflict: these had a great impact in the media and on society as a whole towards ethnic segregation and discrimination. As a result, values such as tolerance, equal opportunity, and respect for diversity did not take root until the second half of the 20th century. However, research with children from minority ethnic backgrounds conducted over the past two decades shows that differences persist in the processes of ethnic self-identification and attitudes among children from minority groups. Some findings even show that young minority children, for example, Africans, Asians, Latinos, Native Americans in the US and Canada, display positive biases to the majority group and negative attitudes to their own group, as well as some confusion about their group membership, a tendency that diminishes by 7 to 10 years of age.

Many researchers wonder whether the extent to which this reduction in prejudice as children approach adolescence may only be apparent, rather than reflecting actual feelings. As they mature, children become aware of socially desirable responses, and they may become more skilled at responding in a socially appropriate fashion. For example, will children display a negative attitude towards the members of an out-group if the interviewer comes from that ethnic

93

group? In a classic study Clark, Hocevar, and Dembo (1980) compared pre-school and school aged children's attitudes to ethnic difference in a situation in which the interviewer was a member of the out-group being investigated. They found differences between pre-school children and older children: the former did not vary their responses according to the interviewer's ethnic group, whilst the latter were more sensitive, providing answers intended not to hurt the questioner's feelings. Does this mean that older children lack ethnic prejudice? It could be simply that older children were aware of the social significance of skin colour and knew the 'correct' answer to give to a member of an ethnic minority. It seems evident that as they grow older children have a greater knowledge of the stereotypes and prejudices that prevail in their particular society (Augoustinos and Rosewarne, 2001), but they also learn more about counter-biases that contradict such prejudices. Further evidence that children are not simply learning to hide socially undesirable prejudice comes from a study that reported no correlation between measures of prejudice and measures of social desirability (Doyle, Beaudet and Aboud, 1988).

The idea that cognitive progress is essential to reduce prejudice comes from cognitive-developmental approaches, and empirical support for this idea is found in several studies that report a decline in bias and egocentric responses at about the ages of 7 or 8. A number of studies (Aboud and Doyle, 1996; Doyle and Aboud, 1995) have shown the relationship between cognitive skills, such as adopting and integrating different perspectives, and the attribution of positive qualities to out-groups. Recent studies on the development of tolerance (Robinson, Witenberg and Sanson, 2001) show that the capacity to accept people with other beliefs or customs develops during the first stages of adolescence, and that this relies crucially on the possession of cognitive skills related to the adoption of multiple perspectives and the reconciliation of opposing points of view. Younger children seem to be less tolerant of ideas that do not match their own or are in opposition to their own.

The development of ethnic awareness among Spanish children

Several European countries like Spain have recently experienced a significant growth in the multi-ethnic nature of their population. Do children and adolescents in Spain show the same tendencies in their developmental of both ethnic identity attitudes towards out-groups? Over the past few years we have conducted developmental studies on awareness of ethnicity shown by Spanish children and adolescents (Enesco and Navarro, 2003; Enesco, Navarro, Giménez, and Del Olmo, 1999a, 1999b; Enesco, Navarro, Paradela, and Callejas, 2002; Gimenez, 1999). These studies are part of two research projects: *Social judgements about exclusion and discrimination towards different ethnic groups: A transnational developmental study* (funded by the Dirección General de Investigación Científica y Técnica de España (BSO2002-05130)) and *Spanish children's stereotypes and prejudices towards ethnic-racial diversity* (funded by the Consejería de Educación, Comunidad Autónoma de Madrid, España (06/0053/2003)).

Adopting a socio-cognitive approach, we examined ethnic self-identification and attitudes shown towards minority groups and the processes of person categorisation. Broadly, our findings show that the development of ethnic awareness follows a very similar sequence to what is described in studies carried out in other multi-ethnic societies, except that the first stages of ethnic awareness appear to develop at a slower pace among Spanish pre-school children. Young children pay little or no attention to skin colour or other racial attributes, although they do use other social categories such as gender and age. This alleged unawareness of ethnic traits is significant in some tasks but not in others, a finding replicated by some other researchers (Ramsey, 1991). For example, in a study carried out with Spanish 3 to 5 year-olds (Guerrero, 2003), they were asked to categorise figures or pictures depicting people with differing skin colour, gender and colour of clothes, and then to choose the figures they most liked. The children's attention to ethnic characteristics varied according to the type of task: most pre-school children categorised the figures by gender or by colour of their clothes but not by their colour of skin. However, when choosing the most liked figure, the vast majority selected white figures. Another study of children's preferences and rejections of pictures representing members of different ethnic groups (Enesco *et al.*, 1999a) found that it was around the age of 4 to 5 years of age that children began to display positive attitudes towards the in-group – and negative attitudes towards out-groups. These attitudes become extremely polarised from 6 to 7 years of age, when preference for members of the in-group and rejection of those of the out-groups reaches its peak. From 8 years of age there is the beginning of a decline in favouritism towards the in-group and rejection of the out-groups. Pre-adolescent ethnic awareness takes the form of a recognition of the social value of being white or Spanish, and an awareness about the social meaning of being a member of a minority group and the consequent effect on life opportunities. Counter-biases that combat rigid stereotypes emerge during this period, and some pre-adolescents claim to identify themselves emotionally with members of ethnic out-groups. This emotional identification is usually associated with judgements against discrimination displayed by other groups.

Studies with Spanish pre-adolescents and teenagers
Stereotypes about a minority group: the case of Gypsies
Spain has a long history of emigration, and much of its experience of immigration is very recent. Over the last six years the number of registered immigrants in Spain has tripled. Before this happened many Spaniards expressed the belief that 'we are not 'racist''. However, this has changed greatly in a few years: the discourse of the average Spaniard is not as it was. What is interesting about this belief in the alleged non-racist attitude of the Spanish people is not simply that it is based on a very limited experience of a multi-ethnic society, but it is how it reveals a very poor awareness of the prejudice that the majority group has actually had – and still has – towards the large community of Gypsies, settled in Spain for many centuries. Though we may speak in the singular about the Gypsy community, there are diverse *romani* groups in Europe, and the differences between them are as large as those between 'Gypsies' and 'non-

Gypsies'. There is much historic documentation about the prejudice and discrimination suffered by Gypsy people in Spain from the end of the 15th century. Forms of discrimination have changed, and we can now identify symbolic racism towards Gypsies rather than institutional racism, as the Spanish Constitution gives the same rights to all, regardless of ethnic origin.

Approximately 450,000 inhabitants of Spain are identified as Gypsies, one of the highest numbers of Gypsies in western European countries. Almost 45 per cent of them live in Andalusia. Various studies of Andalusian adolescents from the majority group have pointed to the strong prejudices these young people have towards the Gypsy community (Galeano, 2003; Gamella and Sánchez-Muros, 1998; Gómez-Berrocal and Navas, 2000; Gómez-Berrocal and Ruíz, 2001). For example, Gamella and Sánchez-Muros studied a large sample of 11 to 15 year-old students' written statements about Gypsies, and they found that extensive negative stereotypes were attributed to them at similar levels in different schools and towns: they were similar to stereotypes held by adults. The most recurrent negative traits were aggressiveness, violence, dirtiness, dwelling in shacks, lacking education and illicit ways of life such as stealing and drug dealing. Fewer positive stereotypes were found: these included traits such as happiness and a talent for singing and dancing. They found that 42 per cent of the students included some of these positive traits in their descriptions, while 80 per cent of them included one or more negative traits. Despite the predominance of negative descriptors, many adolescents also stated – in a rather diffuse way – that 'not all Gypsies are the same', and most did not reject the idea of having a Gypsy as a friend. The vast majority expressed the view that Gypsies had the same rights as everyone else.

The authors suggest that this paradox of simultaneous prejudice and protestations of non-racism, found throughout society, produces cognitive and ideological conflicts that adolescents try to solve through using justifications such as 'I'm not racist but...'. This tactic preserves a favourable idea of themselves which is in harmony with values based on egalitarianism, democracy and solidarity (*ibid*, p 45-46).

Other studies carried out in Andalusia and other regions of Spain (Calvo Buezas, 1990) have found similar results about the type of prejudices towards Gypsies expressed by children and adolescents from the majority group. In a series of studies conducted by our research team (Gómez; González; Paradela, all forthcoming) on the stereotypes and knowledge children and adolescents have about Gypsies and other ethnic minorities living in Spain such as Latin-Americans, Black, Asian, and Middle Eastern people, we have observed that the most negative traits are linked to Gypsies and Moroccans. Both these groups have similar characteristics attributed to them, such as violence, thieving, and *machismo*. On the other hand, stereotypes towards other groups appear to be much less negative and do not convey the same feelings of threat and levels of rejection associated with Gypsies and Moroccans. However, most children and adolescents continue to insist that they 'don't think that way' or that they are 'not racist'. The richest information obtained about stereotypes of minorities was through indirect questions during the interview: direct questioning, such as 'What do you think about Gypsies?' elicited little information, or impersonal responses.

A study of adolescents' judgments about ethnic exclusion

Discrimination and social exclusion based on ethnicity are the origin of many of the conflicts between different groups around the world. Psychologists have invested great efforts over decades to understand the processes of stereotyping and prejudice that underlie these phenomena. However, little research has been done on understanding how individuals reason about social exclusion and discrimination. What makes social exclusion legitimate? Do people offer circumstances in which exclusion is acceptable? How do people reason and justify themselves when they make decisions to exclude someone from a relationship, a group or an institution? These questions are of great interest for developmental psychologists, since it is during childhood that values, rules, beliefs and theories about the social world are acquired and organised into explanatory and evaluative systems.

In the last few years several studies from a social-domains perspective in the United States (Turiel, 1983) have focused on how pre-adolescents and teenagers reason about ethnic exclusion (Killen and Stangor, 2001; Killen, Lee-Kim, McGlothlin and Stangor, 2002). Their purpose was to investigate how students judged the exclusion of a Black child in various social contexts – friendship, peer group, school – and to assess the criteria which are used to justify their exclusion. The researchers anticipated that the context would influence the way they evaluated exclusion, and that they would be more willing to exclude someone from a friendship relationship or a peer group than from school. As expected, it was found that the vast majority of American students between 9 to 16 years of age said that it is wrong for a school to deny access to children because of their ethnic group, supporting this with moral justifications of equal rights and fairness. In contrast, between a third and a half of the students thought it was acceptable to exclude in friendship and peer group contexts, giving personal justifications, such as 'it's up to you to decide who you want to be friends with' or socio-conventional reasons such as: 'the group will not work well with someone who is different'.

We recently conducted similar research, interviewing Spanish students aged 9 to 16 about the possible justifications for the exclusion of a Black or a Gypsy child (Enesco et al, 2002; Enesco et al, in preparation). We were interested in comparing American and Spanish students' reasoning about ethnic exclusion in the same three contexts, and expected that the outcomes would be similar to those of the American students. However, because of the Spanish ethnic composition and the results obtained in previous studies, we hypothesised that our students would be more inclined to accept a Black child than a Gypsy child as a friend or as a member in a peer group.

Contrary to our expectations, practically all Spanish students rejected the possibility of excluding a Gypsy child as strongly as they did the idea of excluding a Black child, making no distinctions between the contexts of exclusion. In other words, they considered it wrong and unfair to prevent either a Gypsy or a Black child from school, as well as to exclude a member of either group from friend-ship or membership of a peer group. Some students even rejected the right to choose their own friends if such a right involved discrimina-tion against a person because of his or her ethnicity. This is remark-able because in other interview situations that make no mention of ethnicity, adolescents affirm their right to choose whoever they like as their friends.

These findings reveal some interesting differences in the way Spanish and American students face ethnic exclusion. Americans are more likely to accept and justify exclusion when it involves only two persons and no basic rights are threatened than they are when a basic civil right, such as the universal right to education, is concerned. In contrast, Spanish students seem to view all these situations as if they were restricting a fundamental right, the right to be treated as a person, independently of group membership.

How should these differences between American and Spanish stu-dents be interpreted? Are Spanish students less prejudiced than Americans? This seems unlikely considering the findings previously discussed. As we have seen, ethnic prejudices are present in Spanish children and adolescents, and their developmental trend is similar to that of children from other Western countries.

The results described in the previous section may help explain these findings on these young people's judgments about exclusion. It is likely that the survey participants were facing a conflict between the negative biases towards the out-group shared by the majority – for example, that Gypsies are not trustworthy – and the social values of tolerance and equal rights. Over the past fifteen years Spanish state schools have developed a curriculum emphasising tolerance and res-pect for diversity, and students seem to accept these ideas as socially desirable. The option taken by the vast majority of Spanish students to reject any kind of exclusion could indicate their desire not to be racist. That the majority of adolescents and adults have very little contact with people from the Gypsy community might suggest that the responses were guided by an ideal image of society and of them-selves, more than by a realistic account of social relationships.

Furthermore, the students in the research were attending schools with no immigrant or Gypsy pupils. It remains to discover the extent to which Spanish students in other social situations – for example, in an ethnically heterogeneous school – would maintain their opposition towards social exclusion.

The differences between the Spanish and the American students might be explained by some socio-cultural variables in countries and their respective experience of ethnic diversity. Whilst the US culture is heterogeneous in many places, it also has a specific history based on slavery. In Spain issues of ethnic exclusion are qualitatively different, and the heterogeneity of Spanish society is a recent phenomenon resulting from immigration over the last few years. This does not mean that issues of exclusion or inter-ethnic conflict do not exist, but it does mean that they do not exist in the same way as in countries with a longer multi-ethnic tradition.

The purpose of our current research is to study the development of stereotypes and prejudices among children and adolescents from both majority and minority groups of Latin-American, Eastern European, and African origin, who attend ethnically mixed schools.

Finally, we have to ask whether children and adolescents in multi-ethnic schools show a different orientation towards ethnic discrimination. Would they be more inclined to support exclusion? To what extent would Spanish adolescents living in contexts where ethnic conflicts might arise maintain their opposition towards social exclusion?

7

Do history and geography teaching develop adolescents' historical and territorial consciousness?

Nicole Tutiaux-Guillon

It is generally assumed that history and geography contribute to the formation of collective identity and citizenship, through developing a common culture and shared social representations of the past and of the world, and through promoting acceptance of responsibility for a common territory and a common future. These outcomes are presumed to be so for history all over Europe, even if Euroclio regretted that 'in history education we hardly ever question the effects of our teaching and often society is not very interested in this question either' (Van der Leeuw-Roord, 1998, p11). Geography teaching now aims at developing European awareness, following the lead of the Council of Europe. It also is thought to help pupils develop responsibility for their surroundings and for the planet, and to stimulate their attention towards sustainable development. On occasion geography and history may contribute to education for co-existence and tolerance (Chevalier, 2000).

These aims are most important for adolescents. Adolescence is a key stage in the process of constructing one's identity as an individual and as a member of a community or communities. It is an important point in the process of recognising one's values, one's legitimate views of the world, of society, and of one's possible role in this world/society. Furthermore, it is the time when young people are becoming more aware of what it means to act as a citizen and are developing more openly critical approaches to politics.

At the same time, several research project findings question whether such outcomes for history and geography are achieved, suggesting that there is a gap between official intentions and the real processes of teaching and learning. These projects analysed what is really taught in the classroom and whether the lessons seemed to be fostering identity and citizenship, and what students memorised, forgot and reshaped. These researches, partly quantitative, partly qualitative, have broadly consistent results. The research can be categorised into three groups:

- Research about the understanding of history and/or geography, and about the attitudes of students towards history or citizenship (Lautier, 1997; Angvik and Von Borries, 1997; Tutiaux-Guillon, 1998; Tutiaux-Guillon and Mousseau, 1998; Tutiaux-Guillon, 2000)

- Research about effective teaching of history and/or geography (Audigier, Crémieux, Mousseau, 1996; Tutiaux-Guillon, 1998; Tutiaux-Guillon, 2000; Clerc, 2002)

- Research about what history and geography teachers say about their subjects and practices (Angvik and Von Borries, 1997; Lautier, 1997; Van der Leeuw-Roord, 1998; Tutiaux-Guillon *et al.*, 2004).

This chapter examines the social and civic aims of history and geography teaching – scrutinising both official definitions and teachers' conceptions – effective teaching and the discrepancies between aims and outcomes. There are some strategies that may reduce these discrepancies. To begin, the two main concepts used in this analysis: 'historical consciousness' and 'territorial consciousness' will be discussed.

'Historical consciousness' and 'territorial consciousness' as goals: what do they mean?

Theoretical approaches to historical consciousness are hetero-geneous (MacDonald, 2000): there is no intention to promote speci-fic historical or territorial consciousness to foster a nationalistic or ethnocentric identity. So 'European historical/territorial conscious-ness' is not used to mean a specific cultural content and attitude to be fostered in Europe: this is part of a political and ethical approach to history education in Europe that is not discussed here (Mac-Donald, 2000). In this chapter, the expressions 'historical conscious-ness' and 'territorial consciousness' are used to identify an attitude or ability to develop social and personal significance related to the past and to space. This is not of univocal or normative significance, and can be built on different levels. Historical consciousness and territorial consciousness are used as heuristic tools to question the links between the history and geography taught and learnt in school and young people's identity and collective involvement. The ap-proach used here does not take into account the complete richness of these concepts but focuses only on the characters that link historical/ territorial consciousness with citizenship and identity. So the quest for truth, which according to Aron (1961) is an important part of his-torical consciousness, is not explored here. Most students, teachers and parents believe that what is taught and learnt in school is his-torical truth, which can be discussed from a political and a didactical point of view. But the conventional consensus in France does not question the matter of identity and citizenship. 'Historical con-sciousness' is not extended to 'historical thinking', as in Martineau (2000), nor is every dimension of territorial consciousness explored.

Historical consciousness

Historical consciousness requires at least a familiarity with some his-tory: a taste for the ancient, for picturesque relics. But beyond this superficial attractiveness, historical consciousness is a consciousness of historical time. It is an awareness of the actuality of the past in present society and of its possible influence on the present. More than this, it is a connection between past, present, and future (Koselleck,

1979; Chesneaux, 1996). Being aware of the aspects and evolution of past societies provides a basis to judge, to choose and to interpret change, and the references needed to chart a future. To consciously imagine a prospective future shapes one's understanding of the past, and gives rise to a more significant meaning to change. Present time is not only the result of the past, but also the moment from which the past is perceived and constructed: relevant and significant events or phenomena are recognised through present problems. This is not a post-modernist attack on historical truth: historians tend towards the truth, even if they know that they will never reach an exact and complete understanding of the past. Their research programmes and their dominant interpretations are the result of their cultural, economical, social and political contexts. Historical consciousness includes the ability to understand that historical enquiries depend on present preoccupations. Historical consciousness also includes the ability to feel oneself as an historical being, and that history has a personal meaning because it shapes one's life: one is an actor in history. This understanding underlay the enquiry *Youth and History in Europe* (Angvik and Von Borries, 1997).

Territorial consciousness

Territorial consciousness is a concept recently developed by geographers, particularly in Quebec (Laurin and Klein, 1999). Territorial consciousness does not refer only to a familiarity with landscapes, or a taste for nature or for the environment. Territorial consciousness invests a portion of space with values and memories and with meaningful social practices, thus transforming it into a 'territory', an area appropriated, practically and symbolically, by a social group. The group and its territory can be related to very different scales: from family to a whole society, from locality to continent or the world. It does not coincide with the frame of one's own personal spatial experience: it is a land where one's own identity is rooted. It can be the national space or the village of one's origin or said to be the group's original place, or a type of landscape: it gives the individual the feeling of being at home, of going back to oneself. The social significances attached to this territory can crystallise on specific symbolic places that encapsulate identity, values, and aspirations, a concept developed by social and cultural geographers and by sociologists, at least in France. Some of these are *lieux de mémoire* [places of memory] but others are places that evoke transcendence or a sense of typicality, such as the German Rhine, the Magyar *Puszta*, the parishes of the *Tromenie* or the *Sognefjord*. Territorial consciousness also includes an awareness of one's responsibility (as individual and as citizen) in the organisation of the territory and for its future. This means not only knowledge of the territory but also of the powers and forces that organise it, and an awareness of the stakes, the possibilities, the uncertainties and the risks.

Grounds for identity

Historical and territorial consciousness are thus to do with identity: thinking of oneself as a historical being, as responsible for a shared territory, rooting one's identity in a past and/or in a land, nurturing collective and individual identity(ies). Historical consciousness is an awareness of belonging to a group that claims a history, an inheritance, a social memory, and which commemorates events figured as a symbolical part of its identity. The belonging can be multiple: an individual can belong simultaneously to a family, a social class, an ethnicity, a nation and a culture. But for these groups, and for individuals who participate in them, the past has a shared meaning, and is valued and appropriated through this meaning. History is uncompromisingly seen as part of social life and references to the past stimulate judgement on what is/was/will be fair, efficient and good. Historical consciousness is thus linked with values and with political consciousness.

In the same way, territory is thought of as essential not only for social and economic life but also for maintaining identity. One does not necessarily have to live in this territory – there are examples of diasporas – but it is necessary to think of the territory as one's own, as a shared responsibility, and as a component of one's personality and belongings. For the group the territory has a shared meaning, and is valued and appropriated through this meaning. Just as has been described for historical consciousness, territorial consciousness is possible on different scales, possibly in a most intricate manner. Territorial consciousness also induces directions and choices for the future: it underlies politics.

Through such definitions, however partial they may be, it is easy to recognise important components of identity, especially of social identity, and some of the foundations for political awareness and action. Historical and territorial consciousness are elements in one's view of the world, and are also foundations for commitment to the community or communities.

Historical and territorial consciousness as aims for history and geography teaching

History and geography are taught to provide students with the resources to understand the past and present world, and to give them the potential to move beyond their own limited experience. Both subjects also carry conceptions and interpretations that are presented to students as natural, legitimate and common. This may contribute to promote a 'one only' legitimate collective identity. Historians of education have for long identified this as an enlightened nationalistic aim in 19th century Europe: in France during the Third Republic, schools had to pass on the capabilities of a citizen, the identity of a Republican and the identity of being French. Textbooks, far more than the official curricula might suggest, produced a discourse aiming at knowing and loving France and the Republic, and at extending universal values, progress and democracy. We do not really know what was taught, even if some official reports during the twenties suggest more pacifism was seen than nationalism. During the 1960s and 1970s, the official objectives changed and focused more on competencies and abilities and during those decades teachers and intellectuals criticised nationalism as being indoctrination. The same intentions – and the same criticisms – were developed in the former communist countries during the 1990s when one key educational problem was to find some form of collective significance for school social sciences.

Official intentions in France

In the 1990s the importance of promoting a common culture and an attachment to democracy was renewed. The diversity of the student body resulting from the increased access of every student to secondary education to at least the end of compulsory school at age 16 was seen as the source of tensions and difficulties that could only be overcome by a common culture. This was set in a political frame, inherited from the Enlightenment and from the French Revolution, where every sense of belonging other than being French is assumed to be private. The aim of citizenship is supposed to be the only common general interest and it is assumed that as a citizen, s/he has no gender, no ethnicity, no religion, no class, and no regional roots. Each citizen is equivalent to every other, as each voter is equivalent to every other. The dominant concept of the 'same school culture for everyone' is strongly linked to this conception of citizenship: it defines the legitimate references that everyone should master in order to understand political speeches and to take part in public debates. Integrating migrants means that in France they – or at least their children – are supposed to become French, not by a process of 'Frenchyfying' but by acquiring the ability to separate their own private identity as migrants from their public identity as members of the body politic. The logical consequence is that they need to be introduced to the common public culture. History and geography are part of this common culture, understood not as being nationalistic or ethnocentric but as the foundation of the body politic (Lenoir, 2002). This is very different from the liberal approach of citizenship that is dominant in Anglo-Saxon politics. As has been consistent since the 18th century, French citizenship is not dissociated from an individual's human identity: being open to the world and to humanity is, officially, part of being French. The school curriculum content has always been open to European history and geography.

The history and geography curricula in France is organised by its contents; these contents are compulsory, only a few case studies being left to the selection of the teachers. The study of selected documents is compulsory in order to foster a common identity: these include, for example, the frieze of *Panathenées*, the *Bible*, the

Qu'ran, *The 1789 Declaration of Civic and Human Rights* and De Gaulle's call of 18 June 1940. This common culture is open to Europe: it includes the palatial chapel in Aachen, and Goya's *dos de Mayo* – which is particularly interesting because the *dos de Mayo* condemns the French imperial occupation of Spain, yet is part of what French students must learn – and includes cultural master-pieces of Islam. Considering the Qu'ran as an inheritance for every student is typical of this new tendency. The explicit intention is to give youth sufficient shared identity to alleviate current social and ethnic tensions and to empower them all for a common future. There is no parallel project within the geography curricula, where the syllabus does not stress the links between citizen or social individual and specific territory, nor does it emphasise any symbolic place. But perhaps the iconography – which not prescribed, but is very similar from one textbook to the next – provides common and shared images of French/European/world spaces. According to Gottmann, common iconography is part of territorial identity; he introduced the term 'iconography' to designate shared symbolic representations of land that nurture national identity (1952). The geography taught transmits a particular view of the world that includes the closest and familiar land, through maps (e.g. planispheres centred on Europe), through photographs (e.g. picturing any metropolis from a developing country as shanty towns contrasting with the central business dis-trict), through geographical concepts (e.g. centre/periphery), through geopolitical analysis, and even through the specific framing of a shot of the landscapes inherited from Vidal de la Blache.

To summarise, there is an official curricula that is aimed at historical consciousness, but it is much less defined for territorial conscious-ness. There is no place in this chapter to analyse this difference, which comes from the recent history of geography as a science and as a school subject. Geography is, for the public, a poor relation to history: it is sometimes confused with the nomenclature of places, or a directory of picturesque landscapes and travels, such as in the *National Geographic* magazine. To most people, economic data are more relevant to understand the world than geographical ones.

It would probably be possible to develop similar analyses of curricula contents in other countries: for example, on the place given to the communist period in the curricula in several eastern European states, because deciding which collective memory the school should pass on is a pressing current problem. And several school geography projects suggest possible changes to promote a more European view (see for example EUROGEO, or http://www.ffzg.hr/seetn.htm).

How can history and geography teaching foster historical and territorial consciousness?

Here I draw largely on the results of the comparative enquiry *Youth and History*, completed in Europe between 1994 – 1995 with students aged around 15 (Angvik and Von Borries, 1997; Lastrucci, 2000). This survey of attitudes towards history was the first made with a large sample of more than 25,000 young people. The results showed that social differences were more significant than national ones. The variable 'interest in politics', for example, was a very reliable predictor of a positive attitude towards history. Even if national tendencies were apparent, European youth displayed largely similar shared social representations of the past and of views of history. A recent replication of this enquiry in Canada has suggested that this may be occidental common sense and not purely a European phenomena (Charland, 2003). I present only some results from the French sample, because I intend to link these with didactic practices in history and geography teaching. We lack European enquiries about how those subjects are really taught.

History has a high status in France, not just with youth, but more generally: historical broadcasts are popular (there is a TV history channel), there are many historical reviews, political speeches are littered with historical references, political caricatures refer to history, even political demonstrations use claims or denouncements from history. French students rated the importance of 'using history to understand the present world' more strongly than the average European students, (3.92, on a scale from 1 to 5; the European average being 3.56). Only the Lithuanian and Russian samples were higher than the French. They were more likely to claim that history helps explain the background of present-day life and problems than most other Europe students (French 3.97, European 3.60). Only the Turkish sample scored higher. And they agreed that 'history aims at orientation for the future' (French average 3.51, European average 3.33). They implicitly recognised the link between past, present and future. A majority said that history gives 'a chance to learn from others' achievements and failures' (average 3.47, European average 3.37), and gives 'examples of what is right/wrong, good/evil' (average 3.42, closer to the European average 3.37). Qualitative research confirms these results (Lautier, 1997; Tutiaux-Guillon, 1998): students aged between 15 and 18 said that they studied history in order to understand and appreciate contemporary society, and to recognise the progress that had been achieved. Some students stressed that the history of the peasants during the *Ancien regime*, or of the workers during the 19th century, was 'their own history': 'we are the people' (meaning a social, not a national group). Their historical consciousness, as well as their time awareness, appears well developed.

But as in every enquiry, a minority did not answer in such positive terms. About 20 per cent to 25 per cent did not think of themselves as historically involved, and said that history was irrelevant to their life and of no interest: to them it was 'only a school subject' (Lautier, 1997; Tutiaux-Guillon and Mousseau, 1998). Not only was their view of history different but their vision of the future was also curtailed: they were less interested in politics or in religion, and their idea of their own future was unclear (Tutiaux-Guillon and Mousseau, 1998). Even the students who linked the present with the past referred to few historical events, such as the French Revolution and the world wars, were vague about dates (so 1789 subsumed the whole Revolution), and history often means only the 20th century. Furthermore, current day events are used more to offer explanations of the past rather than vice versa (Tutiaux-Guillon, 1998).

An example confirms this fragility. For 15 to 18 year olds, Europe has no past other than the world wars and the process of unification in the European Union. When they speak of a common European culture, they refer to movies, music and fashion, rather than to history or ancient art. They ignore the European inheritance. In a questionnaire asking for agreement or disagreement with a series of statements they contrast past and present Europe in terms of: Christianity, few cultural differences, conflict and imperialism versus cultural diversity, modernity, peace, democracy and unemployment. This response was probably accentuated by some of them confusing Europe and the European Union, but it also suggests that youth identify a discontinuity between past and present, and anticipated future. Students from Britain, Germany and Italy gave broadly similar answers (Tutiaux-Guillon, 2000). (Note that the *Youth and History* questions were completed in 1994-1995, and the research about Europe was conducted in 1998.)

The history syllabus taught in school was identical for every student, but their levels of historical consciousness were variable. Students' school achievement is never a relevant variable to explain their attitudes towards history. Relevant variables in this case are social background, personal involvement in politics or in religion, and expectations for the future (Angvik and Von Borries, 1997; Tutiaux-Guillon and Mousseau, 1998; Tutiaux-Guillon, 2000). Care is needed in interpreting these data to avoid confusing causality and correlation; by for example comparing students' level of historical interest with the kinds of teaching that they had, one might conclude that an interest in history is the result of traditional teaching styles (Van Der Leeuw-Roord, 1998); but these traditional styles are more common in those states where political changes have been greatest in the 1990s: this is more likely to have stimulated an interest in history.

One further point is relevant. Most young French people do not claim a national identity. In the *Youth and History* enquiry it was found that although French students were interested in their own country's history (average 3.39, on a scale from 1 to 5), this interest was lower than the European average (3.71). The importance that they attached to their nationality/ethnic group was negative (2.64), when every other country's sample answered positively (from 3.1 to 4.2, European average 3.48) (Tutiaux-Guillon and Mousseau, 1998). When interviewed, most youths referred to their French identity as a chance of birth or of residence. Their identity as French was not, in their opinion, rooted in an attachment to a specific history (Tutiaux-Guillon, 2000).

We have no large-scale enquiry to provide data about the territorial consciousness of French teenagers: there has been no open-ended questionnaire on the symbolic places, or on the values that students associate with their life space, or on the territory for which they claim responsibility. Several studies have pointed to the importance youth give to the environment (Percheron, 1993, Tutiaux-Guillon and Mousseau, 1998), particularly to their condemnation of pollution. But young people were not eager to change their lifestyle to help reduce pollution, which brings into question the extent to which they feel responsible for their environment. The link between symbolic places and territory appears blurred: the same young people could approve of the statement that 'the beauty of monuments and the charm of traditions can only be enjoyed in the right setting' (54.0 per cent) and deny that 'reproduced in a park for tourists, such monuments and traditions lost their true meaning' (59.4 per cent) (Tutiaux-Guillon, 2000).

When questioned about the space they associated with their citizenship, 313 teenagers from the Lyon region answered that they felt citizens first of their town (75.1 per cent), then of France (69.9 per cent), then of their region (62.3 per cent), and finally of Europe (49.0 per cent). This suggests that the two components of their territorial consciousness are the effective life space and the symbolic investment. These components coexist on different scales without apparent tension. This interpretation is supported by other responses in the same questionnaire. Perhaps these different territories are thought of as fitting into each other. In interviews, only a minority of 16 to 18 year old students explicitly perceived the territory as the *terroir* [literally soil, meaning foundations] for their identity. What dominated their knowledge was not what they had learnt in school, but what they experienced: Europe was known from travels, from encounters, from discoveries experience, but not from lessons. Those who had never travelled tended to be more anxious about their future and to feel some anxiety about Europe.

The data is insufficient to draw firm conclusions. But it does raise questions about what is passed on in the classroom. As observed earlier, official aims are less clear in geography than in history. But it is disconcerting that the only explicit references to territorial consciousness, albeit in these very limited enquiries, were to experience and to expectations and rarely to school geography teaching. Neither did historical consciousness appear to depend on achievement in school.

Everywhere in Europe the *Youth and History* survey showed that 'students [did] not totally perceive the goals which teachers [tried] to reach in their history lessons': they rated aims differently and the teachers emphasised the importance of each goal as greater than did the students (Van Der Leuw-Roord, 1998, p 111). Teachers rarely pointed to civic and social outcomes of their work in the classroom.

The limits of ordinary teaching in France: topics and practices

The history curriculum in French schools is organised chronologically, from the ancient world in the first year, to 20th century history in the final year of lower secondary education. In upper secondary school the first year covers key moments in European identity and the French Revolution, and the years that follow deepen the study of 19th and 20th century. Only the 19th and 20th century are taught in vocational classes. This chronological structure is strictly observed by teachers, who hesitate to draw links between past and present, except when the local resources provide monuments, and will not question the past from a present day perspective. Teachers say that they hope that 'some day', 'when the students are grown up', the students will themselves connect present and past (Tutiaux-Guillon *et al.*, 2004).

The geography curriculum, in both lower and upper secondary education, begins with a worldwide study of phenomena such as relief and climate), and issues such as population and development as an initiation to general geography, then devotes one year to Europe and France, and concludes with a geopolitical and geo-economic approach to the world. Understanding the world today

115

underlies every item of content, but the countries and the places studied are always objectified and presented as an exterior for students, teachers and geographers, even when the focus is their own state or region.

School history and geography in France give no place to subjectivity or to values. It is assumed that knowledge is the basis for 'good' values and for public-spirited attitudes. School passes on 'truth' and 'reality' in an approach inherited from Enlightenment and from positivism: truth enlightens the citizen and the responsible social individual. Truth is established by science and differs from both common experience and common sense. Of course, it must be adapted to be suitable for young minds, but without changing the core knowledge. This is a commonly shared representation of school knowledge. From this perspective students' private knowledge and experience of the world, or their opinions, have nothing to do with what happens in the classroom, and do not support legitimate knowledge. 'School truth' must be substituted for these frail and dubious sources of information and opinion. Students themselves subscribe to this kind of legitimation. This conception of school history / geography is not supported by the results of research projects scrutinising these subjects: school history and geography borrow from scientific knowledge – often traditional and sometimes obsolete – and from common knowledge. The contents are also the outcome of school itself: specific kinds of knowledge are taught and learnt without being related to any scholarly or scientific practice.

The knowledge passed on in history and geography lessons tends to be neutral, and this is an epistemological and ethical decision. But this can at the same time be counterproductive. For example, teaching about Europe has a main objective to provide young people with the resources to think, act, and live in a changing Europe, where the process of integration is underway and is being discussed. This objective led to the various Ministries of Education in the European Union countries to decide in 1988 to put greater emphasis on Europe in their school curricula, and for the Council of Europe to develop projects to encourage history and geography teaching about Europe. A quick review of French curricula would conclude that Europe is studied in history every year, and in geography at least four years out of seven. But in classroom practice, teaching about Europe is about teaching facts, not understanding their significance. Europe is either a defined object in geography or as the frame for particular topics in history. The core of the lesson is not about reflecting on the present and the future, but on facts, notions and knowledge that can easily be assessed. This explains why students' historical and territorial consciousness about Europe is not referred to within school knowledge.

Texts, concepts, pictures, even maps are reputed to record reality as it is or was, and support information about what is studied, rather than interpretation. Six teachers, interviewed in 2001, insisted that it was essential to teach realistic geography, transmitting concrete *repères* [markers], even for students aged between 17 and 18 These interviews were carried out in a research project on inheritance as taught through school geography, directed by Clerc (unpublished; some results in Clerc, 2002 and Tutiaux-Guillon, 2003 a and b). Landscapes should be analysed not as a social and symbolic constructs, but as visible relationships between nature and humanity. Students are required to observe, describe and characterise 'reality'. This approach avoids any reflection about the development of attachment to a territory or of personal or social responsibility.

Inheritance is not inherited but selected by contemporary society: only some monuments, texts and other works are endowed with significance and values, and reputedly link the future with the past. In school history, inheritance is seen as inherited from the past, without any present involvement. The monuments, texts and works officially prescribed in the curriculum are only set in the period of their creation, so that the Bible is studied along with the ancient Hebrews, the palatial chapel of Aachen with the Carolingians, and the Qu'ran with medieval Islam. The significance that these inheritances have for current society is not questioned, studied or even evoked. Facts and skills are rated more important than attitudes and values, which are neither 'truth' nor school requirements (Tutiaux-Guillon, 2001).

What is said in a history or geography lesson is mostly said by the teacher, and supposedly gives a true picture of the past or of the world; pedagogical supports are used to give a realistic view of the past or of distant reality (Audigier, Crémieux, Mousseau, 1996; Tutiaux-Guillon, 1998; Clerc, 2002). Teachers aim at delivering consensus core knowledge, but this consensus is not arrived at by discussion but derives from the teacher's authority and the students' faith in her/his discourse. The students' adherence is based in the apparent neutrality of what is taught.

For teachers, this neutrality is inherently part of the scientific status of school subjects (Lautier, 1997; Tutiaux-Guillon, 2003). Teachers in France are mainly trained in their academic discipline for four years and selected on their mastery of academic history or geography. Their pedagogical and didactical training lasts only one year. To maintain silence on values and on social issues is to adopt a deontological and ethical position, in which the teachers avoid indoctrination, respect the students' freedom of thought, and exclude from their lessons any 'private' value (see above about the French understanding of citizenship). They agree that their objective is training for citizenship, but conceive of this mainly as transmitting facts and truth to young people so that they can make informed and enlightened choices. In such a framework teachers do not have an explicit aim of developing historical or territorial consciousness, because they think that this will be a natural outcome of learning history and geography. They often argue that students are too young, and that they cannot see how to practically direct their teaching toward this outcome. Younger teachers even tend to doubt the legitimacy of such an objective, particularly concerning identity, common culture and values. This attitude is reinforced by the priority to teach the entire curriculum, and by the apprehension that they cannot be effective in the area of social and individual identity.

The teachers interviewed by Lautier explained how they structured their approach to history teaching as partly presenting history as information and partly as offering an explanation of present and future (Lautier, 1997). Eight teachers we interviewed in 2002-2003 were very similar (Tutiaux-Guillon *et al.*, 2004): they gave examples drawn from dramatic political news stories such as the French presidential election in 2002, conflicts between Israel and Palestine, and wars in the Balkans, saying that when they explained current political situations to pupils, the past was used either as a directory of analogies or as a list of causes. But the same eight teachers hesitated when asked about the relationship between history and identity. Collective identity was not a usual point of reference for them: identity was normally seen to be individual, not as social or political. Is this the result of the influence of individualism in society? Or does it come from some idea of resistance to nationalism and ethnocentrism? In these interviews, references to citizenship were unclear: there was no reference to citizenship in three of the eight, and brief or unclear references in the other five, apart from the claim for a critical mind. Citizenship was something on the horizon for young people and students were too young to be citizens. Questioned about the place given to social and political aims for history and geography teaching in their lessons, teachers either responded that these aims were utopian, at least for their students, or seemed to be disconcerted because they had not been concerned with these objectives. What they wanted was quiet teaching. Two of them asserted that when the echo of the past was too vivid in the present, as it was in the public talk of a 'Crusade' in the post 9/11 context, they skipped over this and choose another option such as the cross-cultural achievements in Roger II's Sicily. Their justification for this was to avoid any increase of potential conflict between students.

The shared concept of learning that dominates professional culture, also averts consideration of the outcomes of history and geography teaching. Learning is conceived of as piling up knowledge: first the basics (the main facts, key points, generalities) then more detailed knowledge (more examples), and then the crowning political and social significance (the icing on the cake!). This highest point could only be worked on 'when there was time' or 'when students are old enough'. This conceptual framework is quite compatible with both the structure of the curricula and with the representation of history and geography as factual and real information. It is also a very convenient way to organise contents over the year and to select the focus for lessons and evaluation. The approach does not challenge a teacher-centred approach that gives little place to students' reflections.

Conclusion: possible orientations

The school is only one of the intermediaries that contribute to the enhancement of historical or territorial consciousness: it must not be forgotten that media, movies, role-play, literature, tourism, songs and discussions with peers and with family all play a part. But school is a place where young people can confront different approaches and where they can be encouraged to develop critical and rational approaches to myths, falsifications, imagination and information.

Developing historical and territorial consciousness is not an explicit aim for teachers, at least in France. Such an objective contradicts the dominant positivistic view of school subjects and school teaching. But some teachers are very aware that without such explicit aims what they teach has no social meaning and no cultural impact, other than incidental.

In France, we have yet to create methods of training teachers that develop their ability to reflect on objectives and practices, particularly in terms of historical or territorial consciousness. We have offered some experimental sessions to give teachers a practical use for outcomes, so that they develop a problematic approach and choose relevant support and questioning for students. These teachers found that being more aware of such outcomes empowered them professionally (Tutiaux-Guillon *et al.*, 2004). The most effective topics were the current political and social problems that could be easily related to past situations or geographical contexts. The critical question that leads to teaching for interactive reflection is simple: these days most information about the world and the past is learnt outside school; so what can make history or geography teaching useful for young people?

II: Identity development and modernisation

8

Mass media and identity development in adolescence

Eva Kósa

Socialisation and media

During the last decade two remarkable shifts have emerged in the interpretation of the socialisation process, modifying previous approaches and theories. These are the new conceptualisation of the role of the environment and the acceptance of the interactive nature of socialisation. Both are significant when analysing the role of the media in the development of identity. The chapters on socialisation in the *Handbook of Child Psychology* in the 1983 (edited by Mussen) and 1998 (edited by Eisenberg) editions are an illustration of such a shift.

The complexity of the environment

Most definitions describe socialisation as a process by which a person acquires, through different forms of learning, the behavioural rules, norms, values, and the way of thinking of a given culture (Clausen, 1968; Scarr *et al.*, 1983). The primary agents of socialisation – parents, peers, and school – are still traditionally the focus of socialisation theory, and they play a fundamental role in transmitting culture (see Maccoby and Martin, 1983; Parke and Buriel, 1998; Rubin, Bukowski and Parker, 1998). However it is now apparent that they are themselves influenced by broader social-societal factors. There are cultural and societal functions, particularly in modern industrial societies, in which these traditional primary agents cannot, do not, or are not willing to participate (Roberts and Maccoby, 1985). A considerable proportion of norms, behaviours, categories and definitions – all aspects of culture – are not transmitted, or are only partially transmitted, by primary agents. Instead they are passed on through representations at the level of the social system, namely through mass communication and the mass media (Bandura, 1977). At the same time, the media can potentially form and influence other factors that contribute to socialisation and also in turn be influenced by these other factors. Thus the media is in an interrelationship with not only the individual, but also with all the other agents of socialisation (Rosengren and Windahl, 1989).

The interactive nature of socialisation

Socialisation cannot be used as a term that implies a linear process and is not used in this way in contemporary theory and development studies. The individual, influenced by specific agents, acquires approved social norms, roles and behaviour through active participation in the socialisation process from early childhood, a process increasingly understood and acknowledged (see the pioneering work of Bell and Harper, 1977). Some interpretations go further in emphasising individual agency in socialisation, noting the growing role of other influences that undermine the importance of traditional socialising agents. Growing individual freedom to make decisions about activities, leisure and consumer behaviour, style and taste suggest that it is possible to 'biographise' one's own life (Livingstone, 2002). All of these characteristics are particular determinants during adolescence, when autonomy and individual choices are crucial and intensive.

Taking this broad theoretical framework of socialisation, this chapter will discuss the role of the media in the development of identity in adolescence from two perspectives. The first of these focuses on the power of the media to model and influence, which is connected mainly, but not exclusively, with being exposed to the content of the media. The second focus is connected primarily with the context of media use.

Content effects
Socialisation, identification and media

One of the most exciting questions about socialisation is how the socialisation process happens: how does the individual acquire the outer norms, behavioural rules and morality that will be the socialised person's inner guide?

Though shaping, rewarding and punishment are important ways of learning one's culture, many psychological approaches put greater emphasis on the role of modelling and identification as the dominant forms of learning within socialisation. Identification is the process of becoming like another person, 'in both small and large ways' (Scarr *et al.*, 1983, p 551). Parents are prominent models in this process, but the older the child, the more models might be involved. Gestures, behaviours, norms, judgements, attitudes, styles and values are all adopted and become fragments of a unique individuality. Several psychological approaches, particularly Erickson's psychosocial theory, stress that achieving identity is the main task of the adolescent (Erikson, 1963). Identity, the inner self, provides uniqueness and continuity, an awareness of oneself as a distinct person and how one fits into the social world, and acquires a sense of direction.

Adolescents face new social pressures to grow up and behave in a more mature way, building up and maintaining new types of relationships with people from different age groups, of different genders and different social status, while at the same time experiencing many physical changes in their bodies. Their bodies will look and feel different, they will think differently, and they will evaluate events in both their narrower and broader social life in different ways than before (Havighurst, 1972). During all these changes, identity provides adolescents with an integrated blueprint of what they will do with their bodies, their minds, and their relationships (Dacey and Kenny, 1994). The consequence of all this is that adolescence, particularly late adolescence, can be characterised by an intensive search for identity, forcing the individual to ask 'Who am I?'

Teenagers search for ways to be independent and autonomous, and in trying to define themselves they actively seek role models from outside the family as possible alternative choices. The various forms of media depict lifestyles and characters and give young people believable messages about a wide range of factors concerning identity, ranging from gender roles to how to create intimate relationships, from how to get different kinds of gratification to how to cope with stress and how to act as adults. The media give lessons in problem solving, on popularity and on how to be successful. The power of the media to establish and glorify role models – whether they be accepted or rejected – is outstanding. And although the media, especially television provide a 'relatively restricted set of choices for a virtually unrestricted variety of interests and publics' (Gerbner *et al*, 1986, p19), repeated media representations of lifestyles, values, personalities, roles and attitudes suggest that these are widely accepted and successful.

The acceptance and popularity of media role models has been well documented (Arnett, 2002; Bryant and Zillman, 1986; Gerbner, 2000; Bryant and Bryant, 2001; Signorelli, 2001). It is also illustrated by our study of Hungarian adolescents (Kósa, 2002), in which questionnaires were administered in a classroom setting to adolescents of 14 or 15 years of age. The largest proportion of the boys (46 per cent) selected their favourite personal model from the media, and although 41 per cent of girls chose role models from within the family, 33 per cent of them found their models from the world of television. These categories were created based on the sources from which respondents had selected the models. The least popular choice was from school.

Almost every aspect of the development of identity can be affected by the role models provided by the media, and the overwhelming bulk of research on media investigates the consequences of being exposed to certain kinds of media, both its content and its messages. Most of this research has focused on aggression, arising out of scientific and societal concern about increased juvenile crime and delinquency; but there have been other studies of the behavioural and attitudinal effects of exposure to the media (for example, Roberts and Maccoby, 1985; Bryant and Zillman, 1986; Rosengren, 1994; Bryant and Thompson, 2002; Singer and Singer, 2001). The influence of dominant media representation is of particular significance during adolescence.

Gender roles

Gender is perhaps the most significant aspect of identity, developing from the clues given by adults and peers in the first years of life. These reflect the norms and expectations of socially accepted gender behaviour in a given culture, and an early lesson for children is that transgressing these norms evokes negative responses. But the real and adult-like commitment to sex-role behaviour comes during adolescence. Young people keenly observe each particularity of being masculine or feminine, and the media are a constant source of information on this. Content analyses suggests that, apart from some recent changes, the media is traditional, conservative, and male-centred, particularly in the case of television. It is generally found that:

- sex roles are portrayed in highly stereotypical ways and men and women are cast in traditional and heavily stereotyped roles

- men outnumber women in prime time programmes

- females are usually younger and appear in more conventional roles such as mother, wife and lover (Gerbner et al, 1986)

Sex in the media is shown as immediate pleasure rather than mutual acceptance, tolerance and compromise. Youth magazines and music reinforce the view that femininity is based mainly on physical appearance and on the ability to please men (Huntemann and Morgan, 2001). This view might provoke feelings of insufficiency in young people at the beginning of their sexual life (Brown and Steele, 2002). The media also represents the dominance of heterosexual relations between unmarried couples, and seldom gives acceptable role models of non-heterosexual teenagers, relating them primarily to sexually transmitted diseases.

The media are the dominant sex educators for many adolescents. It can be seen that they give a distorted representation of sex roles, and contribute to the maintenance of traditional gender roles and expectations and to problems with adolescents' self-esteem.

Health-related behaviour

The primary focus of research in this field is on the effects on health caused by smoking, alcohol consumption, food advertisements and the portrayal of entertainment in the media. Links between media portrayals and health-related behaviour, such as eating disorders, alcohol consumption, sexual activity, and cigarette and drug use, are widely accepted (Bryant and Thompson, 2002). The influence of the media on adolescents' dissatisfaction with their body image is considerable. The thin body type is shown as ideal for females and the muscular ideal is given for males in the media: these create almost unattainable models for young people. These ideal body types are also portrayed as being essential for achieving success with the opposite sex. Since the media preferred by teenagers – magazines, music videos and television – dominantly project these body-image standards, they increase concerns about physical changes to the body, and teenagers are particularly prone to the risk of experiencing body image dissatisfaction, leading to eating disorders (Dacey and Kenny, 1994; Hofshire and Greenberg, 2002).

Portrayal of minorities

Minority groups in many European countries are not only under-represented or missing in the media, but are also largely portrayed negatively, by being associated with unemployment, crime, violence and drug abuse. Moreover members of such groups are seldom presented in inter-ethnic relationships (Gerbner, 2000; Bryant and Bryant, 2001). Huntemann and Morgan (2001) point to three potential outcomes for minority ethnic young people as a consequence of this:

• they see their own group as undesirable, and this has negative repercussions on their personal ethnic identity, leading to either

• denying their membership of this group, and behaving, looking, and acting as if they were not members of the group, or

• becoming increasingly frustrated at this social exclusion, opposing the majority culture, thus strengthening their attachment to and identification with their ethnic group culture.

It is important to recognise that only the third outcome – of opposition – will reinforce the development of ethnic identity. Though the media often function as cultural and social homogenisers (Kósa, 2002), this also underlines the power of the media to increase alienation and segregation. Although the media claim that they do not create, but only reflect, minority stereotypes, they do play 'a significant role in repeating, normalising, and perpetuating many negative images of specific groups' (Huntemann and Morgan, 2001, p 316). It is clear that the media's potential power to build cultural bridges, to increase multicultural awareness and cultural pluralism, and to show the positive aspects of cultural diversity, is not being utilised.

Work and occupation

Commitment to an occupation is seen as one of the tasks to be accomplished during the transition to adulthood. Without personal experiences of work, adolescents' impressions about occupations come principally from their representations in media. But the world of work as shown in the media is highly stereotyped and limited. The division of work between the sexes is generally shown in traditional ways, men engaged in successful or exciting activities as policemen, lawyers, managers or doctors, whilst women are shown dominantly in domestic or nurturing roles, or in decorative roles assisting men in their adventures. Actual work is hardly ever depicted and the general impression conveyed is that work is about status, power and money, rather than involving hard effort (Signorelli, 2001, Huntemann and Morgan, 2001). The media sustain stereotypes and evoke unrealistic expectations of occupations.

The dominance of these sorts of models amongst young people's role preferences may have considerable consequences, even if there are factors modifying the power of the media. For example, László (1999) found there was greater propensity to select personal role models not shown in the media but from within the family or from teachers at school – depending on the educational level of the father, the religious orientation of the school and viewing less television.

The context of media use

Although these possible effects of the content of the media are fairly widely accepted, these influences are by no means uniform. Those consuming the media may have preferences for different media forms, select different content within those forms, and react in different ways to the same medium form and content. There is an interrelationship between leisure activities, media access, and media use. Similar levels of television viewing can have different effects on someone who is lonely and does little else than view programmes, than on someone who has access to alternative media and many social relationships. This contextualisation is essential if one is to avoid the moral panic that arises whenever a new medium appears. Books and reading are still favourite media forms for some people, in spite of the fears that they would be replaced by comics, or predictions of 'the end of the Gutenberg galaxy': the end of traditional paper-printed media) The context is an ever-widening circle (Bronfenbrenner, 1979) and without paying attention to this there is a danger of applying a technologically-determinist, media-centric approach, perceiving the next generation as couch potatoes, computer-addicts and net-nerds (Greenfield, 1984; Livingstone, 2002). If we are to understand the socialising influence of the media on young people's identity development, the role played by the media in adolescents' daily life should be taken into consideration along with their individual patterns of media use.

Age-related trends in media use

Media use is not used here to mean either media consumption or time given to using a particular medium. Following Rosengren and Windahl (1989), media use is a combination of four different elements: the level of consumption of a given medium, the type of content, the relation of the individual to the selected content, and the context in which the media is consumed. There is no fixed relationship between these elements, so the level of consumption/time cannot be used as an exclusive index of media use. Furthermore, habitual and actual media consumption should be differentiated. When comparing the media-related activities of adolescents with those of younger children, significant differences have been identified:

- the amount of time spent watching television declines steadily through adolescence. Television viewing generally increases during childhood and, apart from a slight decrease when entering school, peaks in late childhood (Roberts and Maccoby, 1985)

- the preference for books, magazines and comics during adolescence shows some decrease but the research data has been controversial (Brown, 1976; Johnsson-Smaragdi, 1983), and shows strong gender differences (Greenberg *et al.*, 1993; Kósa, 2002)

- the use of video cassettes, personal computers, mobile phones and the internet increases during adolescence (Livingstone, 2002)

- films are one of the favourite forms of media for adolescents (Rosengren, 1994)

- the media-content preferences of this age group are distinct from the content preferences of other groups of the population: music is an especially favoured content (Greenberg *et al.*1993; Rosengren and Windahl, 1989).

The reasons for these trends may be because there are remarkable changes in social orientation and involvement during adolescence. Friends and peer groups become increasingly important and act as a reference group in several areas. Although the role and emotional importance of parents and other family members continue to be of significance, when there is an harmonious family atmosphere, adolescents are usually less involved in family programmes, and spend increasing amounts of their leisure time with peers and friends. Television is often a shared family activity: this may be why young people prefer either individual television use, or using media centres more on other, peer-related activities.

A reasonable explanation of these changes is given by the 'uses and gratifications' approach (Blumer and Katz, 1974; Rosengran and Windahl, 1989). According to this, use of the media is governed by the need to achieve satisfaction. Different needs lead to the use of different media, and various preferences fulfil individual motives and gratifications, which also shape the influence of the media. This assumes that individuals actively select both medium and content to gratify their needs.

This gratification approach was the basis of Brown's reorganisation model of how people changed their use of the media (1976). This model suggests that four basic elements have a role in how the media are used:

a) personal needs to be satisfied
b) the content of the media must be suitable to satisfy these needs
c) control over selection
d) the ability to 'read' the medium

Brown postulates that any change in these factors will restructure a child's functional orientation to the media. Control has a specific significance for adolescents. Media such as books, films, magazines, and music are not only more likely to meet their changing needs and provide suitable content, but are also much more under the control of the adolescent when compared to television. The final element – the ability to 'read' the medium – also affects change in media use, and many newer widespread media such as the internet may have age-related characteristics (see Masek in this volume).

These trends were evident in our research with Hungarian adolescents (Greenberg, Brand and Kósa, 1993). We analysed the media orientation of two age groups, 12 and 16 year-olds, and found, in the area of gratification, that television was clearly the source most often cited, in six of the sixteen areas of gratification examined. But when analysed by age, 16 year olds found more media gratification in books and movies, and it was the 12 year olds who found television a very strong source. Gender differences were also strong: boys more often preferred television, while girls found similar satisfaction through books, radio, magazines and newspapers. Another and more recent study comparing Hungarian and Swedish adolescents found similar preferences and gender differences in 15-year-olds (Kósa, 2002).

Personal characteristics

Individual differences can lead to great variation, and may shape both the use of the media and its possible effects. Adolescents' various ways of coping with different aspects of development, activities and social relations may be determinants in this. Heavy media consumption can be a substitute when there are problems in interpersonal relations, whether with peers, partners, parents or other adults. This is evident in both the amount of television viewing and in the time spent by a young person in the virtual world of the internet seeking friends or partners. Problems of social adaptation, having a low level of self-esteem and emotional disturbances are often reported as correlated with particular kinds of media use (Bryant and Thompson, 2002).

Much research has been directed at finding a relationship between media use and personality traits. Various personality constructs, such as extroversion, neuroticism and locus of control, have been examined in relation to media usage and preference, but the results are not clear cut (Wober, 1986). An alternative approach, the 'optimum arousal and sensation seeking theory', assumes that the control of an individual's mood, through the achieving and maintaining of an optimal arousal level, are dependent on the characteristics of a given medium, the aspects of its use, and its mediated content (Bryant and Zillman, 1986). Accordingly, regulation of behaviour is controlled by the actual affective state, and the individual tries to maximise pleasant states, and minimise negative ones, by avoiding negative and seeking and increasing positive stimulation. This is mainly spontaneous, but much of the entertainment provided by mass media is consumed in order to alter moods. Although a large consumption of such media content may have undesirable side effects, such use of media 'can provide highly beneficial emotional experiences, that are truly recreational and may be uplifting' (Bryant and Zillman, 1986, p 321). Adolescents have frequent alterations to their moods, and often use different media intensively – especially music – in order to switch to more positive moods.

However all the characteristics of adolescence are in some way consequences of earlier socialising influences, which still have some power. For example, children with emotional disorders who spent more time with television during their pre-school years are almost certain to watch television much more than their problem-free peers when reaching adolescence (Johnsson-Smaragdi, 1983).

Life-style, youth culture

Visible differences in media consumption are found in terms of gender and social class in this age phase. Some studies in gender differences have already been referred to: here I focus on the effects of social class.

The Swedish Media Panel Program (MMP) carried out by Erik Rosengren and his collaborators gives useful data to illustrate this (Rosengren and Windhal,1989). In the MPP study cross-sectional and longitudinal design were carefully combined, on the assumption that the media's influence on different aspects of human development and functioning can only be detected over the long term: similar assumptions are seen in Gerbner's (2000) cultivation theory. The MPP study suggests that clarification and differentiation is needed in discussing social class. In differentiating class and status, three types of class should be identified: the class of origin, the class of destination, and the class of context. (Rosengren's questions behind these categories were: 'Where do you come from, where are you going, and where are you just now?' (*ibid* p 248) and are particularly germane in adolescence.) Using this differentiation of social class, the conclusions from the analysis of the MPP data were that the influence of the class of origin on media consumption decreases, and the influence of the class of destination increases, whilst the influence of the class of context on media use remains constant during adolescence.

This increasing influence of the class of destination can clearly be connected to adolescents' efforts to find and achieve an identity. Young people building their identity more often choose activities in harmony with their preferred future commitments and characters, leaving behind their earlier, family-tied, determinants.

The individualisation of media use

One of the best examples of active self-socialisation is the way that adolescents use media. They use media to define themselves, and media choices can be the means to express their developing identity in a personal way. Arnett suggests (1995) that this expression of identity is one of the five characteristic media uses of adolescents (the others being seeking sensation, coping, entertainment, and identification with youth culture). Moreover, media use not only defines the identity of the user, but also effectively demonstrates this identity to others. Media and content preferences can mark group membership, creating different subcultures for youngsters, offering clear distinctions from other age groups, from younger groups as well as from adults.

The media no longer structure time, daily activities and routines in the homogeneous way they used to decades ago. They now allow various and diverse forms of uses and choices, over when they are used, the content, and the particular medium: they consequently contribute to establishing various and highly different forms of individuality. This visible shift from dominant forms of media to the availability of multimedia and wide media content adds to and fosters the diversification of lifestyles and individualisation.

The connection between the preferred content of media and personal and social identity is more significant in music, which is a particularly globalised commodity – than is the case for any other media. Music choice, and in many cases sport, are particularly suitable ways of expressing subtle differences in personal preference, lifestyle, and subculture. The rationalisation of particular use or preference given by an adolescent is that of being a fan. Livingstone concludes from his study of 15 year olds, 'fandom is the "glue" which connects personal identity, social and peer relations, and taste-preferences in a media-rich environment' (Livingstone, 2002, p115). On becoming a fan – which is common in adolescence – the use of both older and newer media will be determined by this. The 'market-and-profit-fan' media move quickly to promote fandom: favourites appear in films and videos, on cereal packets, on television, T-shirts and comics. Leisure is turned into consumption, thus integrating individualisation and consumerism (see Thoresen in this volume). Adolescents trying to define themselves as different from the family actively seek many forms of identity confirmation and are thus exposed to an increasingly globally structured market. Although specialisation is particularly important for teenagers, the specificity of this is still linked to social class and socio-economic status. Preferences for popular music are more frequent among working-class young people, while books, personal computer use, and internet use are more popular among youth from higher social classes (Rosengren and Windahl, 1989).

Conclusion

The availability of mass media today, and pre-eminently the ubiquity of television, transforms the process of socialisation into something quite different from previous generations. More traditional media, such as film, magazines, and television, are being supplemented by rapidly developing new technologies, such as videodiscs, broadband access, satellites, and the internet in the daily lives and activities of children and adolescents (see Masek in this volume).

The intensive use of these media and the near-permanent exposure to mediated representations, popular images and symbolic models influences young people's perceptions of reality, social norms and socially accepted behaviour. The massive flow of repeated images accumulate and shape the experience of childhood, affecting attitudes, cognition, both antisocial and prosocial behaviour, emotional states, stereotypes and attitudes, sexuality, the formation of identity and conceptions of reality (Gerbner et al., 1986, Gerbner, 2000; Greenfield, 1984; Roberts and Maccoby, 1985; Singer and Singer, 2001, etc.).

When teenagers actively look for attractive models on whom to mould themselves, they commonly choose them from the media (Kósa, 2002). These models strongly influence how the individual will relate to her /his own body, to their sexuality and to their health. Mass media are thus powerful factors in determining what teenagers think of the world, and how they define, relate, and perceive themselves in relation to it (Singer and Singer, 2001).

Age-related changes in orientation towards the media have further consequences for the formation of identity, related to changes in young people's social, cognitive and emotional requirements. Industrialised societies foster and appreciate autonomy, and young people build and attain their potential through their use of media. Patterns of media consumption are easily recognisable and suitable to become distinctive ways of self-realisation, differentiating them from other age groups, and drawing boundaries between them and other groups who would, in earlier times, have been major determinants in the socialisation process.

As a result of this adolescents prefer other kinds of content, use media for different reasons, and gratify their altered needs in different ways than did earlier generations. Preferences for books and comics decline and interest in films, radio, and popular music increase. While teenagers still devote considerable time to television, their favourite media (magazines, films, music and the internet) are those where they can control the content and the mode of use. Arising from their social orientation toward their peer-group, media-related activities turn from family-related media to peer-related media, creating clearly identifiable subcultures. This seems to be a general trend in industrialised societies, although there are some remarkable differences, between cultures and within a given culture. For example, some Scandinavian research suggests there is less dramatic change in content preference and in media consumption during adolescence (Johnsson-Smaragdi, 1983)).

Are there specific European characteristics in the process of growing up with the media? The answer is twofold.

There are few specific European characteristics as far as the content of the media is concerned. The commercial media are highly globalised and highly Americanised. And, despite common complaints, these are more popular than most of the content produced in national media, particularly in the case of television. If media content is to be used to better advantage, as a mediator of local, national, cultural traditions and to mediate multicultural values, then particular national media companies and policy makers need to exercise responsibility.

More national specificity can be found in European countries when considering the use of the media for self-definition, self-expression and actualisation. Our research data shows that content preferences and the source of role model preferences are rather similar across European countries, but that the media preferences for different kinds of gratification differ between adolescents from different European countries (Kósa, 2002). Leisure time activities, life styles and ways of lives – and within these, the use of media – show more connections to family and societal traditions and to national characteristics, than was thought before. Perhaps the most salient characteristic of European media research is the interpretation and study of media influence within this broader and more complex framework (Johnsson-Smaragdi, 1983; Rosengren and Windahl, 1989 (the Swedish MPP is an unique opportunity for the analysis of such interrelationships); Rosengren, 1994; Livingstone, 2002).

Media are powerful and may provoke fears, but their advantages are far from being fully utilised. Introducing media studies as a curriculum subject into primary and secondary schools in an increasing number of European countries, including Hungary from 2003, is to not only train critical awareness and understanding and to educate wise, selective and critical media consumers (see Thorensen in this volume) but 'to learn the process of personal judgements on which one can act after leaving school, when confronting media daily throughout one's lifetime' (Hogan, 2001, p678). To test the effectiveness of this will be the task of future research.

9

The impact of mediated communication on adolescent's identity and citizenship

Jan Mašek

Adolescents' perception of the world, their experience, values and attitudes have become increasingly determined by technical means of communication. Although '(media)-mediated communication' is not a novel term, referring to communication between participants separated in space and/or time, mediated by interconnecting media, the social sciences have only recently become interested in understanding the characteristics of the new social environments created by electronic communication, and the effects on people, groups and organisations. The new media systems, such as the computer, television, HDTV (high definition television), radio, (video)phone, print media, film, video and cyberspace, include a wide variety of technical systems that enable people to communicate with each other. For example, the generic term 'computer-mediated communication' (CMC) is now commonly used for all communication by means of computer networks (Dills, 1998; Mašek, 2001). Indisputably, all these systems bring a virtual experience in the form of interaction through a machine (Swartz and Hatcher, 1996). Note that we need to distinguish between the term virtual reality, meaning hardware and software configurations that simulate alternative realities (Merrill *et al.*, 1992), and the term experience, meaning interaction with others without the mediation of a machine.

Contrary to the approach of regarding communication as simply information transfer (which separates knowledge from the communication process) we must be aware that it is only possible to communicate if participants have a common ground of shared beliefs, that they have reciprocated expectations, and that they accept rules for interaction that serve as necessary anchors in the development of conversation (Clark and Schaefer, 1989). CMC is thus generating an alternative concept of communication as the shared construction of meanings (Kraut and Streeter, 1995). To specify this kind of communication, the following fundamental features of CMC may be considered:

- The technology has its own social and rhetorical context created by software communication, and particularly the unique social context where participants use reading and writing strategies for the exchange of information

- The notion of answerability: every utterance contains the potential for future reactions or answers and students can respond at any point in the conversation and can contribute to the discussion at any time

- The construction of shared responses: it is possible for individual contributions to be made to a joint activity, and to share disagreements, misunderstandings, conflicts and divergent understandings

In the general context of modelling and discussing such a complex phenomenon as the impact of the mediated communication and virtual experience on the adolescent's development of identity and citizenship, we have to work at both psychosocial and technological science levels. As the problems of mediated communication are very complex, it is only possible to note and describe some of the essential problems and questions.

The technology of mediated communication predominantly uses computer-mediated communication systems and telecommunication networks to compose, store, deliver and process communication. In psychosocial and educational practice, we can mainly discuss and model the following technological aspects of electronic environments (Mašek, 2001):

- Multimodality (multimediality) and the intensity of the recipient's sensation and experience. Both offer certain levels of similarity in the mediation of reality and provide multi-sensory contexts (through the functional integration of text, images, moving pictures, audio and 3D audiovisuals and tactile messages) and emotional impact, depending on the quality of the medium's expression

- Interactivity, as a stimulus to actively respond and provide feedback and as a cooperative component of the communication environment, which encourages reciprocal responsibilities for achieving successful interaction and instigates a series of subtle adaptations among interlocutors.

- Access, distribution and evaluation of media products in a global dimension and the possibility of virtual cross-cultural communication.

- Support in using both asynchronous and synchronous communications.

- The freedom of a communication form that is explored in the open and of non-linear hierarchy-structured messages.

Multimodality and the stimulation of impressions on the recipient

The limitations of this model of the media are evident, but its use allows us to deduce the level of psychosocial quality and the social proximity of media systems, especially cyberspace, HDTV and the Web in social and citizenship communication. The ability to transfer content with features that reflect the emotional and social aspects of humanity and the ability of the media to imitate reality, independently of media content, are especially important.

Based on a technological model, comparing systems with high levels of multimediality, such as television, HDTV, the internet and virtual reality, we may understand the weak position of the web's impressive influence on the recipient (Mašek, 2002). Yet the web does provide multi-format information such as hypermedia, audio, video, text and photo, with a global reach, in ways unmatched by any other combination of media. Because of this, from the psychosocial point of view one should not underestimate the role of poorer media, such as internet-based interactive text communication environments, such as chat rooms, e-conferencing systems and e-mail, in which adolescents can experiment with their own identity and even explore particular social roles.

One-way communication media
The use of non-interactive media in an educational and community environment such as television programmes, radio, audiotapes and videotapes as time dependent media also is significantly importance in adolescents' class and home activities. Here the passivity of the spectator, the possibility of misunderstanding the content of the media, and also the possible problematic impact on education, are well-known problems, which have been much discussed by specialists (Gauntlett, 1995). The most significant problem for young spectators who are lacking in maturity is of correctly interpreting these often complex messages: help may be needed in explaining semantic aspects of the content, including basic concepts and terms. It is important to strengthen or correct influences on adolescents' moral or social behaviour (whether positive or negative) through educational activities with teachers, parents, relatives and other adults. This educative social environment should help discuss and explain moral categories and attitudes, in order to establish basic features of culture and citizenship awareness. Another educational solution using these non-interactive media would be to organise them into structured prosocial and civic educational programmes, such as educational television channels.

Communicating asynchronously and synchronously
Technological services can now offer opportunities to use both asynchronous and synchronous information interchanges, depending on the interlocutor's needs. Asynchronous communication electronic

media can significantly enrich people's potential to communicate. CMC environments offer discussion forums which allow asynchronous dialogues through e-mail, list servers and bulletin board systems, which provide the adolescent with more time to reflect on her/his own ideas and encourage more critical thinking and contributions: this has been analysed in research such as Teaching Graduate Programs Using Computer Mediated Communication (Wiesenberg *et al.*, 1996). This model of communication, carried out in a well-structured, non-spontaneous environment, dominates in contemporary web-based education (Shotsberger, 2000).

On the other hand, synchronous communication provides dialogues in which participants interact with others at the same time but usually in different locations. Here there are more human opportunities to amplify both the responsiveness and the familiarity of the dialogue, both of which are very important for developing identity in the adolescent. Shotsberger wrote that web-based instruction.

> ... design should ensure that all participants have access to a wide range of communication options, both synchronous and asynchronous, that can be used in large group, small-group, and one-to-one settings. (1997, p105)

Looking to the future of mediated communication and the development of communication systems, it may be hoped that such human moments in virtual on-line communications will be fostered. Ensuring a balance between synchronous and asynchronous communication is a hopeful way to enhance the effect of media use on young people's behaviour.

The 'openness' of hypermedia communication space

One exclusive capability of CMC environments is that they offer communication with hypertextual and hypermedia messages, accessible mainly via the internet. Hypertext and hypermedia are methods that enable the creation of, and access to, nonlinear text or media through hypertext links, as connections between text paragraphs, pages and multimedia elements. In the context of the openness of hypermedia messages it must be recognised that the interconnectivity of these links is based on the semantic relationships or mental associations of the author, so the communication that is offered with the freedom of exploring and creating links is always conditioned in an authoritarian way. But the overall advantage is that such non-sequential communication may well, in the constructivist paradigm of education, develop adolescents' abilities through helping them:

- construct their own meaning of experiences, based on what they currently know by, for example, improving a student's understanding of community

- by providing contexts in which the students can access, discover and construct cultural knowledge through an active self- or group-directed learning process

- by offering flexible information resources, supporting natural exploration with structured hypermedia documents such as jumping to other pages or sections within web pages, another powerful advantage online publishing has over classical hard-copy publishing

- by offering an associative, rather than linear, style of document writing, which could revolutionise adolescents' intellectual discourse

In adolescence, hypertext is not considered as a 'disorienting source of information'. According to Tierney *et al.* (1992), hypertext appears to adolescents to make ideas more accessible and has motivational qualities which regular textbooks lack, and user disorientation is not considered as a dominant problem. Suler (1998) describes, in relation to adolescent needs, the online information role of teenagers' home web-hypertext pages, in which they describe themselves.

Global and cross-cultural communication

Global mediated communication depends principally on the internet and on television and radio satellite channels. Unlike the previous one-way communication of television production and broadcasting, the web has distinctive attributes that permit the design and use of unique psycho-social activities:

- stimulating adolescent individuality, by dissolving the artificial wall between the adolescent and the real world: according to Hackbarth (1997, p193) 'students can find original materials and collect first-hand information themselves.' Further, we can say that it is their first point of contact with the world and that much of the content on the web cannot be found in other formats

- providing an easy mechanism for students to make their work public: the web allows the work of each individual to be shared with the world, and the recipients can examine the work of others, which enables global comparisons and collaborations

- allowing on-line global meetings and distribution of electronic materials: hypermedia is a flexible resource students are likely to encounter and rely on in the workplace, and the web provides an easy way to create and distribute multimedia materials

The web creates a virtual culture, particularly in education and entertainment, where it particular fosters the concept of a virtual community, building and networking between participants. It thus serves as an environment for adolescents to engage in discussion with their peers and leading authorities in their field over a wide range of topics, and creates a wide audience for their activities. An example of this use of the internet is described in Dunn and Occhi (2003), which presents a case study of college students from the University of Northern Iowa (USA) and Miyazaki International College (Japan): electronic communication between the two groups made students become more aware of the diversity of experience and opinion within each society. Cross-cultural electronic communication through the internet allowed them to revise preconceived images and to acquire information about the other culture: they also found the information exchange an interesting and important way of learning.

Processes of social and cross-cultural communication are very complex and require systematic media education for adolescents. This should focus on the analysis of creating, selecting and interpreting the community's media message. There is also a need to analyse the media from the point of view of historical, cultural, ideological, business and political constraints (Crawford, 2000): these are impinging upon:

- processes of creating the media and the influence on this exercised by powerful interest groups

- selection of both the media type and the message structure to maximise the desired communication effect

- processes of interpreting the media, related to the ability of the adolescent recipient, and of parents and teachers

Adolescents and the web-mediated communication

To understand the effects of mediated communication – and particularly the effects of the internet – on adolescents, the many psychological aspects of mediated conversation must be acknowledged. Even though the cyberspace environment is of recent origin, this is an area of intense concern for psychologists, as well as for educators and parents.

One of the basic problems of mediated communication is that those participating in it switch their attention from the recipient to the problem and content of the message. This leads to a reduction in the normal hierarchy of real life – of the status and roles of those communicating – and of those engaged in mediated communication who often unconsciously transmit their feelings, fantasies and fears to those with whom they communicate (Turkle, 1988). The impacts of CMC on intra-familial communication are also significant: Bold (2001) suggests that negative aspects include acting as a substitute for family interaction, leading to isolation and decreased communication between family members. Positive aspects might be increased communication with distant family members, facilitating shared learning between generations, closing the gap between parents and adult children, and increasing parent-child communication.

The internet environment offers a variety of psychosocial pheno-mena and problems and this is becoming increasingly attractive, particularly to adolescents. The fact that the user is anonymous, the limited type of communication, multimodality, the elimination of potentially distressing social situations, the lack of fear from dis-closing personal information: all these powerfully weaken accepting social roles during the interaction (Kiesler *et al.*, 1984). This lessen-ing of the effect of social rules, and the transformation of some internet services to environments in which users may act without social deterrence leads to the creation of a 'disinhibited environ-ment' (Šmahel, 2003). The adolescent user easily acquires a kind of anonymity for her or his behaviour, as though being a part of a crowd. Such a crowd suppresses the effect of human individuality and leads to what Gustav Le Bon (Joinson, 1998) describes as the phenomenon of 'deindividualisation'. Research by Joinson (1998) examined the various degrees of openness shown by questionnaire respondents, and found that when asked to answer via the internet, they showed less anxiety than when asked to answer on paper. Suler (1998) presents the following needs and motivations of adolescents who often surf the internet:

- identity experimentation and exploration: in the context of cyberspace, adolescents are grappling with who they are, and can find some of the answers

- intimacy and belonging: during adolescence young people experiment with new intimate relationships, especially with the opposite sex, looking for comrades and new groups. These relationships are a major part of exploring one's own identity. On the internet they can find many people and groups with varied personalities, backgrounds, values, and interests. Same-sex gay identities may also be explored more easily in the anonymity of cyberspace

- separation from parents and family: adolescents often seek independence and want to be separate from their parents. The internet is an exciting place to fulfil those needs, especially when their parents know almost nothing about the internet

- venting frustrations: adolescence can be a difficult and irritating period because of pressures of school, family and friends. Young people can vent these frustrations – especially those of a sexual or aggressive nature – in the anonymous world of cyberspace

Another motivation is adolescent sexual activity through cybersex, particularly in the form of writing: 'they describe in detail what they do to each other and how they feel' (Suler, 1998). Access to related visual information may then cause complications, which may stop free imagination.

The possibility of exploring social skills is no less important. The adolescent who spends considerable time chatting on the internet will improve her/his on-line social skills, particularly the ability to communicate with a wide variety of people.

Web-based text environments are attractive places to realise adolescents' needs. For some young people, the attractive feature of e-mail communication is that you cannot see or hear the other person. The adolescents confide in anonymity and therefore in safety, and act differently and more confidently. There is also the stimulation of a high level of fantasy and expectancy on the part of the interlocutor. Internet services, e-mail or e-mail lists (also known as listservs) and discussion groups (newsgroups) are frequently utilised as flexible and powerful means of communication. Frequent e-mail exchanges can shape complex emotional relationships and the space in which the adolescents live together.

Asynchronous communication in chat rooms and instant messaging are among the favourite services of many teenagers; they may also communicate with each other in real time. These are now among the most used internet services and the subject of much research. In his analysis of adolescent talk in a chat room, compared with real conversation, Šmahel (2003, p 108) found out that virtual talks:

- stayed unfinished in the majority of cases: the respondent ended the conversation in mid-topic for various reasons and virtual talks often ignored other possible topics for conversation

- lasted much longer than real and finished conversations: even when the respondent gave real talk undivided attention and did not talk to others, the duration of virtual talk was four times longer

- contain shorter and bare sentences: adolescents often express opinions and feelings in a condensed way, with short sharp answers leading to more questions and greater activity during the chat. This would probably not be necessary in real conversation

- led in some cases to more accurate formulations, as though the internet encouraged the ability to express oneself concisely and accurately

Computer technology and chat systems in particular offer the possibility of the multiplicity of communication, in which the adolescent communicates with several people simultaneously, often in different communicative environments. Some adolescents indulge in this quite intensively, though generally they do not understand its superficiality and imperfection. It is questionable whether this kind of communication offers them a form of relaxation, sport or a distraction from their own problems. From a psychological view, one might talk of the 'dissociation' of the personality, the young person projecting their fantasies, imagination, unconscious tendencies, wishes and complexes on to their dissociated identities in the virtual world.

The use of multi-user virtual environments (MUVEs) and MUDs (Multiple User Dimension/Dungeon/Dialogue) offer complex fantasy worlds, in which adolescents create imaginative roles and scenarios. At present these environments are often based on text communication (Suler, 2000), and might be compared to a living novel, complete with characters and plots, or to a very sophisticated party with its own idiosyncratic rules and culture. In multimedia environments such as Palace (Suler, 1998), the text dialogues occur in a visual room and the participants use visual icons called avatars to represent themselves; some adolescents identify themselves imaginatively by changing their name, age, identity, or gender. Another variation is to use a video camera and microphone during communication as video-conferencing but the technological demands make this a less common form for adolescents. Suler (1998) suggests that the environment of video-conferencing is not as much fun for adolescents as anonymous and/or fantasy-based cyber-space.

Mediated communication presents a contradiction. Although adolescents regard the virtual relations as illusory, and realise the superficiality and short-duration of such relations, they plunge into various forms of virtuality and mediated communication, where they often get a feeling of acceptance and emotional support.

Citizenship education use of media

Just as the role of media in helping form adolescents' identity is increased by the changing nature of technology, we can observe how the media enhance and support possibilities for citizenship education. Adolescent identity may be discussed through various approaches, from 'sharing a variety of family and community values and cultural heritage through intellectual and emotional experiences individuals and groups', while conceptions of ethnic or national identity, closely linked to citizenship and citizenship education, are also bound to cultural identity (Delgado-Moreira, 1997).

In general, young people's social behaviour and citizenship, including their citizenship education, is increasingly influenced by media information sources and citizenship related e-discussions with software simulations. A third area in this context is the use of media to enable students to produce citizenship-related cultural products. This is potentially the most interesting way of using ICT for citizenship education, and fits closely with 'developing skills of enquiry and communication'.

The use of media as a source of citizenship information has become vitally important. The offer of so many disparate databases, hypermedia documents and world wide web resources has been welcomed by educationalists as a ready source of citizenship information. ICT facilities significantly contribute to the curricula objective of passing on 'knowledge and understanding about becoming informed citizens' to students and in stimulating them to take an interest in society. Buckingham considers it important for educators and researchers to avoid seeing this increased access to citizenship media resources as necessarily leading to increased levels of citizenship awareness:

> Theoretically, [research studies] adopt a notion of political socialisation that is highly functionalist: young people are seen as passive recipients of adults' attempts to mould them into their allotted social roles. The approach here is thus essentially psychologistic. Young people's disaffection from politics, for example, is seen as a kind of psychological dysfunction caused by a lack of information, rather than the shortcomings of the political system itself: all we have to do is provide the information and disaffection will disappear. (1999, p173)

As well as online and networked communication packages which include e-mail, chats and videoconferencing, there is another citizenship use of ICT in the stand-alone simulation package. Typically, such software is based on citizenship simulations of social situations, often in narrative form. Citizenship simulation involves presenting various scenarios, in which the student is required to make decisions and judgements at regular intervals. This use of media and interactive communication to develop empathetic discussion and decision-making is now a standard model of current citizenship education software design (Selwyn, 2002).

Adolescents' media communication activity, based on the production of cultural products, such as their own text documents, websites or videos focusing on citizenship issues, could be time-consuming and expensive. But the process of active design and production offer a more valuable learning experience than the passive consumption of the finished books, articles or film. The ethnographic research project VideoCulture (Niesyto and Buckingham, 2001) focused on the potential of audio-visual media production as a way of communicating between young people from different cultures, and it provided a case study of the potential outcomes and limitations of using media production with secondary school students in Germany, Hungary, the Czech Republic, England and the USA. Student awareness that their films were to be viewed by students in other countries was seen as an important element of the project's success. The young people were often found to be highly innovative producers of video programmes, but they were less active as audiences. They learned a great deal from producing their own materials, and were critical and often dismissive reviewers of the work of others.

In the context of the enlargement of the European Union, the adolescent's feeling of identity and solidarity within an individual European nation and in the context of a potential European identity implies an important discourse about European citizenship (Delgado-Moreira, 1997). There are a variety of projects and discussions around European topics, for example in the 'Association des Etats Généraux des Etudiants de l'Europe' (AEGEE). This is an interdisciplinary student association, involving students and young graduates in supporting the communication and integration of academic environments across Europe. The media design dimension of this is promoting the project AEGEE.tv (the European Internet television station for young people in Europe) (AEGEE-Europe, 2004). Over 50 students and young professionals are experimenting with creating television: this offers the possibility for young people from all over Europe to share their ideas and experience.

All these features and areas of mediated communication could be developed to form a valuable supplement to existing citizenship approaches, as a part of developing an inclusive, participative and values-led model of citizenship education.

Conclusion

All media – including the world wide web – can excite adolescents' approaches to cultural, moral and national identity and citizenship and together they offer a great variety of virtual experiences. Modern media, particularly cyberspace and the world wide web, are leading to deep interactions between teenagers' explorations of their identity and citizenship communication and education, and increasing moral and cultural consciousness. However, this increased awareness is likely to be shallow, because the mediated communication implies, unlike real and face-to-face communication activities, a number of questions. To carry out a complex analysis of mediated communication and ICT issues, we must be aware of the following issues:

- the ability of mediated communication to imitate reality and provide other specific features of computer communication environments

- the social implications of media, both for individuals and at the societal level

- the influence of social, cultural, political and economic factors on the shaping of technology and communication processes

- questions of equity of access to and use of the media and issues of power and control associated with all new media and technologies

- the historical precedents of mediated communication, as well as the future potential of the new technologies

The virtual experience may be an important facility in citizenship education and identity in the future. We should neither underestimate it, nor elevate it over other ways of communication. Excessive use of mediated communication can lead to dissipating the communicative potential of all media, including the internet.

10

The development of consumer identity in adolescents in Europe

Victoria W Thoresen

The same as before – only different

The socialisation of today's adolescents is in principle similar to the processes most young people have experienced throughout history. Adolescents strive to express their own individuality, to establish their independence and to define their own purpose in life. First and foremost, they test out ways of interacting with others, in order to discover which function best. However the world today is a new world in the sense that the conditions affecting socialisation differ significantly from those of even the previous generation, and the consequences of the choices adolescents make are often more serious and far-reaching than ever before. Individualism has a more dominant position in society while, paradoxically, activities based on concepts of regional and global solidarity also blossom (see Villanueva and Onate in this volume). Technological innovations and globalisation have created a generation of cosmopolitans, jet-setters, immigrants, refugees, corporate cousins and world citizens, all of whom must deal with the challenge of defining who they are in terms of constantly changing criteria and increasing commercial pressure. Geographical, biological, political, economic and historical factors are no longer key determinants of identity for today's young people in Europe.

Tangelo or onion?

There are those who maintain that young people of today have multiple identities, segmented like a tangelo, which is a hybrid of the tangerine and grapefruit (*pomelo*). Others contend that, as with Ibsen's Peer Gynt and the onion he peels away to nothing, the postmodern person actually lacks a basic identity altogether and constructs her/his identity as circumstances allow.

> [Peer Gynt addresses the onion]
> I'm going to peel you now, my good Peer!
> You won't escape either by begging or howling.
> [Takes an onion and pulls off layer after layer.]
>
> ... What an enormous number of sheaths!
> Isn't the kernel soon coming to light?
> I'm blessed if it is! To the innermost centre,
> It's nothing but sheaths – each smaller and smaller -
> Nature is witty!
> (Henrik Ibsen, *Peer Gynt*, Act V, Sc.5)

To comment on the development of consumer identity in adolescents in Europe, the various categories which have been established concerning identity formation must be considered.

David Reisman (1950 and Walter Truett Anderson (1997) claim that traditionalists (sometimes called social-traditionalists) are those who have a solid and lasting identity, an internalised set of values, based on religious, cultural, professional or other codes. Neo-romantic individuals also have identities that are internally controlled, but their fundamental principles spring from a nature-inspired wisdom. The logical rational individual has, as the source of her or his identity, external controls, such as expertise, facts and all that defines objective normality based upon modern scientific analysis.

Another category of externally controlled identities are those formed by interaction with other individuals and groups. An increasing number of researchers during over decades (for example, Mead, 1928/71; Goffman, 1959; Mauss, 1985; and Geertz, 1983) acknowledge principles of social construction that emphasise the importance of social interaction on identity building. An individual is seen more as a product of his/her social relationships than as the result of her/his original characteristics. Thus role models and social/commercial influences are considered to have a particularly strong influence on the construction of identities.

The classification of individuals in this way distinguishes characteristic traits of different social groups, which assists in determining what influences identity formation. But this also implies a simplification of the human condition. The complexity of the social creature, man, is reflected in the fact that most individuals have both internally and externally influenced identities and therefore fit into several of the above categories. The traditionalist is not necessarily immune to the influences of social interaction and constructs many aspects of his/her personality and lifestyle on the basis of these. The logical rationalist may allow scientific evaluations to determine much of her/his developments in life while still harbouring fundamental religious, cultural or professional codes. Thus adolescents today should be seen neither as onions nor as tangelos but rather as something in between, something embodying a generous portion of traditional social values acquired during childhood but struggling to function in a system where commercial enterprises invest billions to convince them to construct identities based on their products.

To be or to buy?

The central question is why commercial influence on identity is now more dominant than in previous times. What has contributed to the adoption of identities which are so closely bound to the market? Analysts, including Pierre Bordieu (in Parker, 2001), David Miller (1995), David Hollinger (1995) and Richard Rorty (1989), have described many factors affecting individuals' identities in modern society. Many of these are related to or include a degree of commercial activities. The accessibility of commodities, the proximity of other lifestyles, the availability of money, and comprehensive flows of information are factors which need closer examination.

More to things than meets the eye

Commercial identities are externally controlled, despite the fact that they may spring from deeper psychosocial needs. Individuals adjust to new fashions and react to new impulses for many reasons. They may crave, for example, confirmation, social acceptance, status or power. Consumption has become increasingly symbolic, as explained by Baudrillard's reference (1998) to conspicuous consumption or Ernest Sternberg's more recent use of the term of 'icon economy' (1999). Symbolic consumption involves the use of commodities to express personal preferences to confirm one's individuality. Both young people and adults make a point of indicating their social, ecological or political references by what they eat, wear or how they travel.

Criminal behaviour and drug addiction also fall into the category of identity-creating consumer related activities. The desire for power, control, revenge or excess is often a motivating factor. Worldwide crime rates increase on the average by over 5 per cent yearly. Complaints filed in 2003 show an increase of almost 28 per cent from 2002. Forty-two per cent of these relate to identity theft. Internet related fraud accounted for 55 per cent of the reported complaints. The total consumer losses in connection with these exceeded 400€ million. Shoplifting accounts for yearly losses of approximately €13 billion.

Marlboro Man

Due to the advancement of information and communication technology, commercial as well as cultural symbols are transported to all corners of the globe to a degree never experienced in former decades. Rituals, language, ideologies, politics and images of commercial role models no longer belong to one nation or region. This diffusion of symbols greatly influences identity formation. James Duesenberry (1940, quoted in Lancaster, 1991) examined how consumption behaviour is influenced by the lifestyles of respected people and celebrities. Theories about people wanting to keep up with the Jones are still valid. Today's archetypal identities are often described in commercial terms rather than in terms of political success, ideological astuteness or intellectual achievement. According to the numbers of cigarettes and records, films and monogrammed clothes sold, it is figures like the Marlboro Man and Britney Spears who appeal to European adolescents.

Made in Hong Kong

Global production patterns have caused dramatic changes in the lifestyles of masses of people around the world. A wide variety of products now fill the shelves in European shops. Adolescents are tempted by choices their parents could hardly dream of. Food, clothing, entertainment and technology from around the globe are accessible and at affordable prices. The lower costs of production, which has contributed to affordable prices, is due to the work of farmers, peasants, fishermen and tradesmen who have become the modern proletariat. The factories of this global industrial working class, whose owners may sit in USA or Japan or Europe, are spread throughout the world. The products they make are often invisible to the workers themselves as they only produce parts to be assembled at a later stage, but the results are marketed and available to almost every European adolescent. These products can represent the kind of person an adolescent is trying to become or simply be features of hedonistic enjoyment without necessarily bearing any other underlying message.

Today Belgium-tomorrow Burkina Faso

New production patterns combined with technological advances in transportation and communication have led to an increasingly mobile population. Urbanisation, tourism, student exchanges and migration, both for humanitarian and economic reasons, are characteristic of today's European society. The pull of the city and the lure of adventure are not only marketed commodities but also common behaviour patterns of family and friends. As Max Weber (1983) described in his research on achieving status in society, the sharing of a common lifestyle based on consumer behaviour patterns is a key element in determining one's identity. According to Weber, identity formation is determined more by consumption than by income or

wealth. An individual's basic principles and values are com-
municated by her/his consumption. In a similar manner, consumption shows which social groups one aspires to belong to.

Money here, money there, money absolutely everywhere
International exchanges and electronic banking systems have also
contributed greatly to the growth of commercial identities. Money is
the common denominator which makes it possible to compare a vast
number of services and commodities. It is no longer necessary to
have a pile of cowrie shells in one's pocket or a cow in tow to fulfil
one's needs and acquire one's objects of desire. It is no longer just
adults with permanent jobs who have funds to spend on luxury
items. Norwegian adolescents (13 to19 year olds) spend an average
of € 270 monthly on personal consumption. Wherever they go, cash
is easily accessible or credit cards are useable. Loans for personal
consumption are easy to get. Total consumer debt in 2003 rose 12
per cent in the UK and the number of personal bankruptcies in
Germany rose from 13,000 in 2001 to 34,000 in 2002.

Public passions
To acquire an identity it is essential to have information. Young
people seek to know what is 'in' at a given time and what is expected
and approved of by his/her peers. The modern media-dominated
information society provides European adolescents with data which
function as building blocks of identity (see Kósa in this volume).
Common frames of references have evolved due to television, films
and the music industry. This tendency is intensified by market investigations. A young person's private life has become a matter of
public interest in the past few years. Markets collect and analyse
information on what they buy, read, and use money for. Easily
accessible statistical registers indicate where they travel, their health
history, and how much they earn. Market profiles provide fuel for
new trends. Even the media has begun exposing private identities to
the public eye through the popular virtual reality programs.

One of the crowd or a non-conformist?

Commercial identity can be considered as mass produced similarity of expression. It can also be defined as an individual's attempt at achieving authenticity by using commonly accessible indicators in particularly personal ways. Today's society is paradoxical in that it is characterised by continually increasing diversity while at the same time exhibiting more conformity and stereotypes than ever before. This is commonly referred to as the dilemma of homogenisation and differentiation (Goffman, 1992). The world is at the same time both larger than it was and smaller. The consequent shifting of loyalties and redefining of goals have occurred both on collective and personal levels. In this sea of diversity, people are adrift and searching for ways of indicating who they are. Commercial markets exploit this uncertainty to convince future customers that their product reflects the values and attitudes the customers are looking for. To maintain profits and continue selling, companies must nurture insecurity and create discontent in order to keep customers buying.

> From 1950 to 1990, total global advertising expenditure increased nearly seven times. It grew one third faster than the world economy and three times faster than world population. ..... Ads in fiercely competitive OECD markets are now mostly about establishing brand loyalty and evoking human desires, dreams and lifestyle options. (OECD, 2001, pp7-8)

Creolisation

Arjun Appadurai (1990) refers to factors mentioned above, describing five dimensions of global cultural flow. He calls these ethnoscape, technoscape, finanscape, ideoscape and mediascape. Due to this cultural flow, individuals construct, to a far greater extent than previously, their own environments and demonstrate their own uniqueness without the support of their original cultural patterns and symbols. Cultural pluralism does definitely still exist. Nonetheless there are increasing indications that international creolisation is rapidly taking place and that this creolisation is highly influenced by the media and the market.

Creolisation is the process of adaptation and integration of cultural norms and values that occurs when two or more cultures come in close contact. Adolescents in Europe come not only into close contact with one culture, but with a large number of cultures and traditions. In terms of time spent exposed to cultural influences, European youth are more exposed to commercial influences than anything else. If one excludes the time in school, the amount of commercial messages transmitted by radio, television, newspapers, films and advertising dominate the time and space left over for other forms of messages in the day of most European young people. Constant exposure to commercial influences leaves definite psychosocial impressions on young people. To what degree this occurs is a highly debated theme in media research. But the integration of commercial stereotypes with cultural archetypes in the formation of the identities of European adolescents is inevitable.

Commercial creolisation can be seen across the globe. Joining in a common youth movement directed by market forces, adolescents unite to emphasise that they are, in fact the new generation.

> In a world divided by trade wars and tribal conflicts, it is the teenager, of all people, who represents the new uniting force. From the steaming playgrounds of Los Angeles to the fancy boulevards of Singapore, youth show an amazing similarity in taste, language and entertainment. They all have on their Levis, dance to Red Hot Chilli Peppers, and hammer away on their computers. Driven forth by such mighty couriers as MTV, new trends spread with magical speed. Youth hear the rhythms of drums an entire continent away, absorb them and make them their own. (*Fortune Magazine*, quoted in Anderson, 1997, p55)

It is, however, questionable whether commercial creolisation provides an enduring base for identity formation or is merely an ephemeral expression of momentary market demands. To have an informed opinion on this matter requires reflection on the burdens and benefits of consumer identity.

Burdens and benefits of consumer identity
Puppets of the market
European youth must constantly make decisions in relation to the modern consumer society, choosing between a vast variety of possibilities. The risk involved in making the wrong choice has proven to be sometimes devastating. Anxiety and irresponsibility grow. Lifestyle illnesses are more common and serious. Anorexia and bulimia, for example, are frantic efforts to fit into the accepted market-borne picture of a typical teen. Chronic lack of sleep, a widespread lifestyle condition affecting adolescents in many parts of Europe, concerns doctors because of the consequences for the individuals' health, welfare and ability to function in society. Diabetes and overweight brought on by unbalanced intake of sugar and lack of physical exercise are considered by the World Health Organisation (2003) to be one of the major problems of adolescents today. Some young people who choose to go their own way have experienced the stigma of individuality to be so heavy that they cannot face the challenge. Worldwide, one million people commit suicide yearly. As many as 450 million people worldwide suffer from mental health or behavioural illnesses. There is a documented increase in life-style related suicides amongst adolescents in Europe. Drug addiction increases. Drug trafficking globally constitutes an estimated €85 billion every ycar (greater than the GNP of three-quarters of the 207 economies in the world).

Burdens accompanying commercial identities are not only related to mental and physical health. Debt is a recurring problem for many adolescents in Europe, particularly caused by excessive use of mobile phones and slot machines games. Household debt has increased significantly and steadily in the USA and Europe in the last ten years. The accumulation of worn out mobile cell phones, computers and music equipment has created environmental dilemmas. Media-induced violence has resulted in repeated tragedies, not only in the USA but in Europe as well. Media-stimulated fixation on sex has, according to experts, contributed to the increase of international child pornography leagues and sexual abuse of children. The list of negative consequences of consumer-oriented identities is long. But

161

the picture is not entirely dismal. Consumer identity has also proved to be positive and creative for the individual and society.

Critically aware consumer-citizens

Many European adolescents have taken their consumer identity seriously. Previously the conscientious consumer focused first upon value for money, then consumer rights, and finally environmental and health and safety issues. Today young consumers are concerned with civilising the market economy and contributing to sustainable development, in the social, economic as well as ecological sense of the phrase. The complexity of modern society and the immense amount of information available make this a formidable task. Distinguishing their own values and norms from those of the market, some have developed skills for acquiring and interpreting relevant knowledge as well as for making critical choices in the marketplace. The diagram below indicates the central elements considered when making responsible consumer choices (Thoresen, 2002; Steffens, 2002).

Elements of responsible consumer choice

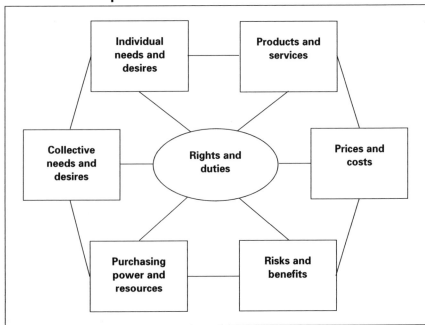

Additional questions the conscientious consumer asks are: which systems and processes must be maintained, and which are defective and in need of alteration? What is the individual's role in relation to the larger mechanisms of the society? How can she or he influence production, marketing, sales, pollution and recycling? Which rights and responsibilities exist and which are lacking?

These and similar questions lead to determining what type of consumer identity adolescents choose. Consumer identity can be someone concerned with maintaining a lifestyle of:

*   *Appropriate consumption*: based on deep and broad debate about the type and level of consumption practiced and whether quality of life, particularly in civic, cultural and religious terms, is increased or impeded by consumption behaviour and its effects

*   *Conscientious consumption*: based on realising more quality of life and less environmental cost through more considered choosing and using on the part of educated consumers

*   *Responsible consumption*: consumption which provides mutual benefits for the producer and the consumer, for those affected by the processes, and for waste and energy use

*   *Collaborative consumption*: consumption which includes actions such as leasing, repairing, sharing and recycling

    Based on UNEP, *Consumption Opportunities*, 2001

There are few statistics to date confirming or denying the extent of consumer citizenship exercised by European adolescents. In 2000 UNESCO and UNDP carried out a study of 8000 adolescents in 24 countries enquiring about the hopes and interests young people had and how concerned they were about ecologically and ethically responsible consumption. The results indicated that adolescents at that time did not see many connections between their personal behaviour and global problems. Nonetheless, evidence exists that adolescents are involved in the increasing demand for ecologically friendly products, campaigns for fair trade, alternative lifestyles based on sharing and leasing, and participate in debates focusing on sustainable consumption and global solidarity. Concern with improved life quality, which is after all the stated goal of sustainable development, has intensified as have the number of initiatives attempting to contribute to this.

World citizen?

The positive aspects of consumer identity, as described above, are closely connected to the awareness of the interrelatedness of processes and consequences in modern day society. Sustainable development is a global goal. Adolescents in Europe who express a positive consumer identity through their lifestyle choices are making a commitment to a new world order, a more just global economic- and social system. This raises the question of whether there actually is a universal global identity beneath the trappings of shifting commercial conventions? Is it impossible to imagine that the positive aspects of consumer identity are contributing to the emergence of a global identity of the world citizen?

Notes on contributors

Louise Archer is a Reader at the Institute for Policy Studies in Education, London Metropolitan University (UK). She is author of *Race, Masculinity and Schooling: Muslim boys and education* (2003) and is co-author of *Higher Education and Social Class: issues of exclusion and inclusion* (2003). Her research centres around issues of ethnicity, gender and social class and education. In addition to Muslim young people's identities, her research interests include: achievement, aspirations and schooling among urban and inner-city adolescents, British Chinese pupils' identities and aspirations and issues around widening participation in higher education.

Ileana Enesco is a Associate Professor of Developmental Psychology at the Universidad Complutense de Madrid (Spain). Prior to her current appointment she was a Visiting Scholar at the University of California, Berkeley where she became familiar with the research done by Professor Turiel. Her empirical research has focused on the development of moral reasoning, socio-economic concepts and ethnic-racial notions in children and adolescents. She has co-authored several texts and monographs: *El mundo social en la mente infantil* (The social world in the child's mind); *Moral, desarrollo y educación* (Morality, development, and education), *La comprension infantil de la organización social* (Children's understanding of the organisation of society).

Becky Francis is Reader in Education and Deputy Director of the Institute for Policy Studies in Education, London Metropolitan University (UK). Her research interests include the construction of gender identities, feminist theory, and gender and achievement. Her sole-authored books are *Boys, Girls and Achievement; Addressing the Classroom Issues* (2000), and *Power Plays* (1998). She and Christine Skelton are also editors of the readers *Investigating Gender: Contemporary Perspectives in Education* (2001) and *Boys and Girls in the Primary Classroom* (2003). She is editor of the journal *Gender and Education* with Christine Skelton.

Márta Fülöp is a Senior Research Fellow and head of the Comparative Cultural Psychology Group in the Institute for Psychology of the Hungarian Academy of Sciences, Budapest and in the Department of Social and Educational Psychology of the Eötvös Loránd University, Budapest. She is the president of the Social Psychology Section of the Hungarian Psychological Association. She co-edited *Young People's Understanding of Economic Issues in Europe* (2002) and *Pszichológia és Kultúra* (Psychology and Culture) (2003). She has been a member of the Steering Group of CICE since 2000.

Éva Kósa, Ph.D. CSc, is an Associate Professor of Developmental Psychology at the Eötvös Lorand University (ELTE), Budapest, Hungary. She also worked for the Association for Teacher Education in Europe (ATEE, network of Commission of the European Communities) on the inclusion of the European dimension in teacher training, in 1989-94. Her research interest is in social-societal determinants of socialisation process, focusing on the role of media. She participated in national and international research projects, and is co-author of *Media-effects on Personality Development.* She is a member of the editorial board of the Hungarian journal *Applied Psychology* and president of the Media Committee of the Ministry of Education.

Jan Mašek is Doctor of Philosophy (PhD) in Pedagogy with a focus on Media Education, a graduate of Charles University in Prague; and presently a Senior lecturer at the University of West Bohemia in Plzeň, Czech Republic. His research interests are in the fields of Media Didactics, Media Communication and Educational Technology. He has written about thirty papers published in Czech Republic and abroad. He is the Czech National Coordinator for the Cice Thematic Network and was a main coordinator and participant in many scientific and special projects. His most recent monographs are *Audio-visual communication of educational media* (2002, ZCU) and *Open technology in education* (co-author and editor, in press).

Alejandra Navarro is an Associate Professor of Developmental Psychology at the Universidad Autónoma de Madrid in Spain. Her main area of research is related to children's ideas in different social domains: economic (social inequality, socio-economic mobility, work), political (national identity), and ethnic-racial awareness (ethnic-racial attitudes, social reasoning about discrimination, prejudice, and stereotypes). Her current research deals with children's and adolescents' ethnic prejudice towards different ethnic-racial groups living in Spain. The more recent publications (with Enesco) are: *El desarrollo de actitudes y prejuicios étnico-raciales* (The development of ethnic-racial attitudes, and prejudice), and *The development of ethnic-racial awareness during childhood. Implications for school practice* (in press).

Concepción Maiztegui Oñate is a psychologist and Senior Lecturer in the Department of Education, University of Deusto, Bilbao, Spain. Her main research interest focuses around the areas of community development with special attention to the empowerment process linked to socio-educational policies. She has conducted several intervention studies with different target groups including children and women. She is a member of the Multicultural group at the Department.

Alistair Ross is Professor of Education at the London Metropolitan University, UK, where he is the Director of the Institute of Policy Studies in Education and the International Coordinator for the CiCe (Children's Identity and Citizenship in Europe) Thematic Network. His research interests are in the area of the school curriculum (*Curriculum: Construction and Critique*, 2000), children's social and political learning, the careers of teachers (co-editor, *The Crisis in Teacher Education*, 2002), citizenship education, and access to higher education (co-author, *Higher Education and Social Class*, 2003). He is series editor for *European Issues in Children's Identity and Citizenship*.

Victoria Wyszynski Thoresen is Assistant Professor in Education at Hedmark University College in Norway and project manager of the Consumer Citizenship Network. She has specialised in curriculum development, global education, peace education, value-based education, lifelong learning and consumer education. In addition to many years of experience as a teacher and teacher trainer, she has been a member of the Norwegian board for the revision of the country's core curriculum. She is a member of the National Committee for consumer education. She has written textbooks for schools and teacher training and has functioned as an international educational consultant. She has been project leader of several Nordic and European projects. She is also head of the board of the Norwegian Peace Center.

Nicole Tutiaux-Guillon is a Senior Lecturer in the University Institute for Teacher Training in Lyon, and a fellow in Paris 7 University in France. She has a PhD in history didactics and has conducted researches in the field of teaching and learning history, geography and civics since 1990. She has published several books and numerous articles in this field. Her recent books *Youth and History, Europe, political intent and school topics* (with Mousseau, 2000) and *Identities, memory, historical consciousness* (with Nourrisson, eds, 2002).

Maria Villanueva is a Lecturer in Human Geography and teacher trainer at the Universitat Autonoma of Barcelona (Spain). She is currently involved in European projects on citizenship and intercultural education and in an international research on geography in education. Among her publications are *La Unio Europea, societat i territori* (1999); *European integration, Social change and the training of teachers in Spain* (2002) and *Fronteras, identidades y diversidad: un ejercicio de re-lectura del mapa político de Europa* (2004).

References

Aboud, F. and Amato, M. (2002) Developmental and socialization influences on intergroup bias, in Brown, R. and Gaertner, S. (eds) *Blackwell Handbook in Social Psychology*, Vol 4: Intergroup Processes. Oxford: Blackwell.

Aboud, F. E. (1988) *Children and prejudice*. Cambridge: Basil Blackwell.

Aboud, F. E. and Doyle, A. B. (1996) Does talk of race foster prejudice or tolerance in children? *Canadian Journal of Behavioral Science*, 28. pp 161-170.

AEGEE-Europe (2004) *What is AEGEE? European Students' Forum Association des Etats Généraux des Etudiants de l'Europe (AEGEE).* Available on http://www.karl.aegee.org/aegweb.nsf/Full/About.

Ahmad, F. (2001) Modern traditions? British Muslim women and academic achievement. *Gender and Education,* 13, 2. pp 137-152.

Ahmad, F. (2003) Still 'in progress'? – Methodological dilemmas, tensions and contradictions in theorizing South Asian Muslim women, in Puwar N. and Raghuram P. (eds) *South Asian Women in the Diaspora.* Oxford: Berg.

Alexander, C. (2000) *The Asian Gang.* Oxford: Berg.

Allport, G. W. (1954) *The nature of prejudice,* Cambridge, MA: Addison-Wesley.

Alsaker, F., Flammer, A. (1999) *The adolescent experience: European and American Adolescents in the 1990s.* London: Lawrence Erlbaum Associates.

Anderson, W. T. (1997) *Det Nye Selvet.* Oslo: Aschehoug Forlag.

Ang, I. (2001) *On not speaking Chinese: Living between Asia and the West.* London: Routledge.

Angvik M. and Von Borries B. (1997) *Youth and History, a comparative European survey on historical consciousness and political attitudes among adolescents.* Hamburg: Körber Stiftung.

Anthias, F. and Yuval-Davis, N. (1992) *Racialized boundaries: race, nation, gender, colour and class and the anti-racist struggle.* London: Routledge.

Appadurai, A. (1990) Disjuncture and Difference in the Global Cultural Economy, in Featherstone, M. (ed) *Global Culture.Nationalism, Globalization, and Modernity.* London: Sage. pp 295-310.

Archer, L. (1998) The social construction of identities by British Muslim pupils aged 14-15 years. Unpublished PhD thesis, University of Greenwich.

Archer, L. (2001) Muslim brothers, black lads traditional Asians: British Muslim young men's constructions of 'race' religion and masculinity. *Feminism and Psychology,* 11, 1. pp 79-105.

Archer, L. (2002a) 'It's easier that you're a girl and that you're Asian': interactions of 'race' and gender between researchers and participants. *Feminist Review*, 72. pp 108-132.

Archer, L. (2002b) Change, Culture and Tradition: British Muslim pupils talk about Muslim girls' post-16 'choices'. *Race, Ethnicity and Education*, 5, 4. pp 359-376.

Archer, L. (2003) *Race, Masculinity and Schooling: Muslim boys and education.* Buckingham: Open University Press.

Archer, L. and Francis, B. (forthcoming a) Challenging classes? Exploring the role of social class within the identities and achievement of British Chinese, for publication in *Sociology*.

Archer, L. and Francis, B. (forthcoming b) 'They Never Go Off the Rails Like Other Ethnic Groups': Teachers' constructions of British Chinese pupils' gender identities and approaches to learning, for publication in *British Journal of Sociology of Education*, 2005.

Archer, L. and Yamashita, H. (2003) Theorising Inner-city Masculinities: 'race', class, gender and education. *Gender and Education* 15, 2. pp 115-132.

Arnett, J. (1995) Adolescents' uses of media for self-socialisation, *Journal of Youth and Adolescence*, 25, pp 519-534.

Arnett, J. (2002) The Sounds of Sex: Sex in Teens' Music and music videos, in Brown, J. and Steele, J. (eds) *Sexual teens, sexual media*. Hillsdale, NJ: Lawrence Erlbaum. pp 253-265.

Arnett, J. J. (2002) Adolescents in Western Countries in the 21st Century, in B. B. Brown, Larson, R. W. and Saraswathi, T. S. (eds) The World's Youth. Cambridge: Cambridge University Press. pp 307-343.

Aron, R. (1961) *Dimensions de la conscience historique*. Paris: Plon.

Audigier F., Cremieux C., and Mousseau M. J. (1996) *Enseigner l'histoire et la géographie au collège et au lycée, étude descriptive et comparative*. Paris: INRP.

Augoustinos, M. and Rosewarne, D. L (2001) Stereotype knowledge and prejudice in children, *British Journal of Developmental Psychology*, 19. pp 143-156.

Augoustinos, M. and Walker, I. (1995) *Social cognition: An integrated introduction*. London: Sage.

Ballard, R. (1994) *Desh Pardesh: The South Asian Presence in Britain*. London: Hurst.

Baltes, P. B. and Nesselroade, J. R. (1972) Cultural change and adolescent personality development: an application of longitudinal sequences. *Developmental Psychology*. 7, 3, pp 244-256.

Bandura, A. (1977) *Social learning theory*. Englewood Cliffs, NJ: Prentice-Hall.

Baudrillard, J. (1998) *The consumer society: myths and structures*. London: Sage.

Baxter, S. and Raw, G. (1988) Fast Food, Fettered Work: Chinese women in the ethnic catering industry, in Westwood S. and Bachu P. (eds) *Enterprising Women. Ethnicity, Economy and Gender Relations*. London: Routledge. pp 58-75.

Bell, R. Q. and Harper, L. V. (1977) *Child effects on adults*. Hillsdale, NJ: Lawrence Erlbaum.

Blumer, J. G. and Katz, E. (eds) (1974) *The uses of mass communication: current perspectives on gratification research*. New York NY: Sage.

Boehnke, K. (1999) Is there social change? Photographs as a means of contrasting individual development and societal change in the New States of Germany, in Silbereisen, R. K. and von Eye, A. (eds) *Growing up in Times of Social Change*. Berlin: Walter de Gruyter.

Bold, M. (2001) Use of computer-mediated communication by families, *Texas Association of Family and Consumer Sciences Research Journal*, 1(6) pp 8-9.

Botcheva, L. (1997) The gains and losses of Bulgarian youth during the transition from socialism and democracy, in Nurmi, J. E. (ed) *Adolescents, cultures, conflicts. Growing up in contemporary Europe*. New York NY: Garland Publishing.

Bourdieu, P. (1990) *The Logic of Practice*. Cambridge: Polity Press.

Brah, A. (1992) Women of South Asian Origin in Britain: issues and concerns, in Braham, P., Rattansi, A. and Skellington, P. (eds) *Racism and Antiracism: Inequalities, Opportunities and Policies*. London: Sage/Open University.

Bronfenbrenner, U. (1979) *The ecology of human development*. Cambridge, MA: Harvard University Press.

Broughton, P. D. (2004) Muslim pupils face ban on headscarves, *The Daily Telegraph*. January 7 2004.

Brown, B. B.and Larson, R. W. (2002) The Kaleidoscope of Adolescence, in Brown, B. B., Larson, R. W. and Saraswathi, T. S. (eds) *The World's Youth*. Cambridge: Cambridge University Press.

Brown, J. D. and Steele, J. R. (eds) (2002) *Sexual teens, sexual media*. Hillsdale, NJ: Lawrence Erlbaum.

Brown, J. R. (1976) Children's uses of television, in Brown, J. (ed) *Children and television*. London: Collier Macmillan. pp 116-136.

Bryant, J. and Bryant, J. A. (eds.) (2001) *Television and the American family. 2nd edition*. Hillsdale, NJ: Lawrence Erlbaum.

Bryant, J. and Thompson, S. (2002) *Fundamentals of media effects*. Boston MA: McGraw-Hill.

Bryant, J. and Zillman, D. (eds) (1986) *Perspectives on media effects*. Hillsdale, NJ: Lawrence Erlbaum.

Buaras, E. A. (2003) German court rejects headscarf ban, *The Muslim News,* 174(31) October 2003: http://www.muslimnews.co.uk/paper/index.php?article=1358.

Buckingham, D. (1999) Young people, politics and news media: beyond political socialisation, *Oxford Review of Education*, 25(1-2) pp 171-184.

Burman, E. and Parker, I. (eds) (1993) *Discourse Analytical Research*. London: Routledge.

Calvo Buezas, T. (1990) *¿España racista? Voces payas sobre los gitanos*, Barcelona: Anthropos.

Csapó, B., Czachesz, E., Liiceanu, A. and Lázár, S. (1999)Being a Minority: Hungarian Adolescents in Transylvania, Romania. in Alsaker, F, and Flammer, A. (eds) *The Adolescent Experience: European and American Adolescents in the 1990s*. Mahwah, NJ: Lawrence Erlbaum.

Castells, M. and Tubella, I. (2003) *Els reptes socials i educatius. La societat xarxa a Catalunya*. Barcelona: UPC.

Chan, Y. M. (2000) Self-esteem: a cross-cultural comparison of British-Chinese, White British and Hong Kong Chinese Children, *Educational Psychology*, 20(1) pp 59-74.

Charland, J.-P. (2003) *Les léèves, l'histoire et la citoyenneté, enquête auprès d'élèves des régions de Montréal et de Toronto*. Québec: les Presses de l'Université Laval.

Chau, R. and Yu, S. (2001) Social Exclusion of Chinese People in Britain, *Critical Social Policy,* 21, (1). pp 103-125.

Chesneaux, J. (1996) *Habiter le temps*. Paris : Bayard editions.

Chevalier, J. P. (2000) La géographie dans les programmes scolaires en Europe, in *Cybergeo*, 129, 15 March 2000, http://www.edunet.tn/hg/ressources/chevalier1.htm.

Chisholm, L., Büchner, P., Krüger, H., Du Bois-Reymond, M. (1995) (eds) *Growing up in Europe: Contemporary Horizons*. Berlin: Walter deGruyter.

Christiansen, F. (1998) Chinese Identity in Europe, in Benton G, and Pieke, F. (eds) *The Chinese in Europe*. Basingstoke: Macmillan.

Clark, A., Hocevard, D. and Dembo, M. H. (1980) The role of cognitive development in children's explanations and preferences for skin color, *Developmental Psychology*, 16(4) pp 332-339.

Clark, H. H. and Schaefer, E. F. (1989) Contributing to discourse, *Cognitive Science*, 13. pp259-294.

Clark, K. B. and Clark, M. K. (1947) Racial identification and preference in Negro children, in Maccoby, E., Newcombe, T. and Hartley, E. (eds), *Readings in social psychology*. London: Methuen.

Clausen, J. A. (1968) *Socialization and society*. Boston MA: Little , Brown and Company.

Clerc, P. (2002) *La culture scolaire en géographie*. Rennes: Presses universitaires de Rennes.

Coleman, J. C., Hendry, L. B. (1999) *The Nature of Adolescence*. London: Routledge.

Connolly, P. (1998) *Racism, Gender Identities and Young Children: Social Relations in a Multi-ethnic, Inner-city Primary School*. London: Routledge.

Connolly, P. and Neill, J. (2001) Constructions of Locality and Gender and their Impact on the Educational Aspirations of Working Class Children. Paper presented at Addressing Issues of Social Class and Education: Theory into Practice Conference, University of North London, London, June.

Coupland, D. (1991) *Generation X: Tales for an Accelerated Culture*. New York NY: St Martins Press.

Crawford, K. (2000) The ideological and political role of the school textbook in constructing national memory, in Ross, A.. (ed) *Developing Identities in Europe: Citizenship education and higher education*. London: CiCe. pp 239-252.

Crawford, K. and Foster, R. (2001) Education for Citizenship in Romania and the UK: A comparison. *Children's Social and Economic Education*. 4(3) pp 170-183.

Csapo, B., Czachesz, E., Liiceanu, A. and Lazar, S. (1999) Being a minority: Hungarian adolescents in Transylvania, Romania, in Flammer, A. and Alsaker, F.D. (eds) *The adolescent experience: European and American adolescents in the 1990s*. Mahwah, NJ: Lawrence Erlbaum.

Dacey, J. and Kenny, M. (1994) *Adolescent development*. Madison WI: Brown and Benchmark.

Davies, B. (1989) *Frogs and Snails and Feminist Tales*. Sydney: Allen and Unwin.

Delgado-Moreira, J. M. (1997) Cultural citizenship and the creation of European identity, *Electronic Journal of Sociology* available at http://www.sociology.org/content/vol002.003/delgado.html.

DfEE (Department for Education and Employment) (2001) Black and Indian Students: improvement in GCSE results. *Press Release* No.2001/0033. London: DfEE.

Dills, Ch. R. (1998) The Table of Specifications: A Tool for Instructional Design and Development, *Educational Technology*, 38(3) pp 44-51.

Donald, J. and Rattansi, A. (eds) (1992) *Race, Culture and Difference*. London: Sage.

Doyle, A. B., and Aboud, F. E. (1995) A longitudinal study of white children's racial prejudice as a social-cognitive development, *Merril-Palmer Quarterly,* 41. pp 209-228.

Doyle, A., Beaudet, J. and Aboud, F. (1988) Developmental patterns in the flexibility of children's ethnic attitudes, *Journal of Cross-Cultural Psychology*, 19. pp 3-18.

Duckitt, J. (2001) Reducing prejudice: An historical and multi-level approach, in Agoustinos M. and Reynolds, K. (eds) *Understanding prejudice, racism, and social conflict*. London: Sage.

Dunn, C. D. and Occhi D. J. (2003) *Contesting cultural representations: Using Internet-Mediated Communication for Cross-Cultural Education*. available on http://www.eastern.edu/publications/emme/2003fall/dunn_occhi.html.

Dwyer, C. (1998) Contested identities: Challenging dominant representations of young British Muslim women, in Skelton T. and Valentine, G. (eds) *Cool Places: Geographies of Youth Cultures.* London: Routledge.

Dwyer, C. (1999) Negotiations of femininity and identity for young British Muslim women, in Laurie, N., Dwyer, C., Holloway, S. and Smith, F. (eds) *Geographies of New Femininities.* Harlow: Longman.

Edley, N. and Wetherell, M. (1997) Jockeying for position: the construction of masculine identities, *Discourse and Society,* 8. pp 203-217.

Edye, D. (2002) Attitudes towards European Union citizenship in Roland-Levy, C. and Ross, A. (eds) *Political learning and citizenship in Europe.* Stoke on Trent: Trentham Books.

Eisenberg, N. (ed) (1988) *Handbook of Child Psychology*, 5th edition. New York NY: Wiley.

Elzo, J. (2000) *Juventud vasca 2000.* Vitoria-Gasteiz: Gobierno Vasco, Departamento de Cultura.

Elzo, J. (ed) (2002) *Los valores de los vascos y navarros ante el nuevo milenio: Tercera aplicación de la encuesta europea de valores.* Bilbao: Universidad de Deusto.

Enesco, I., Killen, M., Navarro, A. and Guerrero, S. (in preparation) *Social judgements about ethnic exclusion: A study with Spanish and U.S. children and adolescents.*

Enesco, I. and Navarro, A. (2003) El desarrollo de actitudes y prejuicios étnico-raciales, in Pardo P. and Méndez, L. (eds) *Psicología de la educación multicultural.* Madrid: UNED.

Enesco, I. and Navarro, A. (2004) The development of ethnic-racial awareness in childhood. Implications for school practices, in D. Hall, L. Leavitt and N. Fox (eds) *Social and moral development: Emerging evidence on the toddler years,* Johnson and Johnson Pediatric Institute, LLC.

Enesco, I., Navarro, A., Giménez, M. and Olmo, C. (1999a) Génesis de la conciencia racial: Un estudio sobre identificación y actitudes hacia el color de piel en niños de 3 a 11 años, *Estudios de Psicología*, 63-64. pp 3-20.

Enesco, I., Navarro, A., Giménez, M. and Olmo, C. (1999b) Developmental processes in children's racial awareness, poster session presented at the 29th Annual Meeting of the Jean Piaget Society, México.

Enesco, I., Navarro, A., Paradela, I. and Callejas, C. (2002) Spanish children's and adolescents' judgments about ethnic exclusion: the case of gypsies and Africans, Poster session presented at the 32nd Annual Meeting of the Jean Piaget Society, Philadelphia, PA.

Epstein, D., Elwood, J., Hey, V., and Maw, J. (eds) (1998) *Failing Boys?* Buckingham: Open University Press.

Erikson, E. (1963) *Childhood and society.* New York NY: Norton.

Estradé, A. *et al.* (2002) *Joves i valors: Els joves catalans en l'enquesta europea de valors.* Barcelona: Col.lecció estudis, Generalitat de Catalunya.

Ferrer G. F. (1999) *Joves i participació a Catalunya.* Barcelona: Generalitat de Catalunya. Secretaria de joventut.

Flanagan, C. A. and Botcheva, L. (1999) Adolescents preferences for their homeland and other countries. in: Flammer, A., Alsaker, F. (eds.) *The Adolescent Experience: European and American Adolescents in the 1990s.* Mahwah. NJ: Lawrence Erlbaum.

Flanagan, C. A., Campbell, B., Botcheva, L., Bowes, J., Csapo, B, Macek, P. and Sheblanova, E. (2003) Social Class and Adolescents' Beliefs about Justice in Different Social Orders. *Journal of Social Issues.* 59(4) pp 711-732.

Flanagan, C.A., Bowes, J. M., Jonsson, B., Csapo, B. and Sheblanova, E. (1998) Ties that bind: correlates of adolescents' civic commitments in seven countries. *Journal of Social Issues.* 54(13) pp 1-9.

Foucault, M. (1978) *The History of Sexuality: An Introduction*, Volume 1, Harmondsworth: Penguin.

Foucault, M. (1980) *Power/Knowledge: Selected Interviews and Other Writings 1972-1977.* New York NY: Pantheon.

Francis, B. (2000) *Boys, Girls and Achievement: Addressing the Classroom Issues.* London: RoutledgeFalmer.

Francis, B. and Archer, L. (2004) British-Chinese Pupils' and Parents' Constructions of the Value of Education, forthcoming in *British Educational Research Journal.*

Francis, B. and Archer, L. (forthcoming) Negotiating the Dichotomy of Boffin and Triad: British-Chinese Pupils' Constructions of 'Laddism', forthcoming in *Sociological Review.*

Fülöp, M. (2002) Competition in Hungary and Britain perceived by adolescents. *Applied Psychology in Hungary,* 2001/2002, pp 33-55.

Fülöp, M. and Berkics, M. (2003) Socialisation for coping with competition, winning and losing in two societies: Hungary and the UK, in Ross, A. (ed) *A Europe of Many Cultures.* London: CiCe.

Fülöp, M., Davies, I., Berkics, M., Hutchings, M., and Ross, A., (2002) Ki a jó állampolgár Magyarországon és Nagy-Britanniában? (Who is a good citizen in Britain and Hungary?) in Gocsál, Á. (ed) *Identitás és Pedagógia. (Identity and Education)* Pécsi: Tanoda Alapítvány.

Fülöp, M., Roland-Levy, C., and Berkics, M. (2004) Economic competition perceived by French and Hungarian adolescents, in Ross, A. (ed) *The Experience of Citizenship.* London: CiCe.

Furnham, A., Kirkcaldy, B. D. and Lynn, R. (1994) National attitude to competitiveness, money, and work among young people: first, second, and third world differences, *Human Relations,* 47(1) pp 119-132.

Galeano, B. (2003) Prejuicio hacia los gitanos. Un estudio piloto con niños y niñas andaluces, unpublished pre-doctoral dissertation, Universidad Autónoma de Madrid, Spain.

Gamella, J. and Sánchez Muros, P. (1998) *La imagen infantil de los gitanos: Estereotipos y prejuicios en escuelas multiétnicas.* Valencia: Fundación Bancaixa.

Gauntlett, D. (1995) Moving Experiences. Understanding Television's Influences and Effects. *Academia Research Monograph:* 13. London: John Libbey.

Geertz. C. (1983) *Local Knowledge: Further Essays in Interpretive Anthropology.* New York: Basic Books.

Gerbner, G. (2000) *A média rejtett üzenete.* Budapest: Osiris Kiadó és MTA-ELTE Kommuni-kációelméleti Kutatócsoport.

Gerbner, G., Gross, L., Morgan,M. and Signorelli, N. (1986) Living with television: The dynamics of the cultivation process, in Bryant, J., and Zillman, D.(eds) *Pespectives on media effects.* Hillsdale, NJ: Lawrence Erlbaum. pp 17-41.

Ghuman, P. A. S. (1994) *Coping With Two Cultures: British Asian and Indo-Canadian Adolescents.* Clevedon: Multilingual Matters.

Giddens, A. (1991) *Modernity and self-identity: self and society in the late Modern Age.* London: Polity Press.

Gillborn, D. (1990) *'Race', Ethnicity and Education: teaching and learning in Multi-Ethnic Schools.* London: Unwin Hyman.

Gillborn, D. and Gipps, C. (1996) *Recent Research on the Achievement of Ethnic Minority Pupils.* London: HMSO.

Giménez, M. (1999) El desarrollo de la conciencia racial: Actitudes e ideas implícitas en niños de tres a seis años, unpublished doctoral dissertation, Universidad Autónoma de Madrid.

Giner, S. (ed) (2000) *Enquesta de la regió de Barcelona*. Barcelona: Institut d'Estudis Metropolitans i Regionals.

Goffman, E. (1959) *The Presentation of Self in Everyday Life* (originally Edinburgh: University of Edinburgh Social Sciences Research Centre, 1956), revised and expanded edition. New York: Anchor Books.

Goffman, E. (1992) *Vårt rollespill til daglig: en studie I hverdagslivets dramatikk*. Oslo: Pax Forlag.

Gómez, M. (in preparation) El desarrollo de la conciencia étnico-racial en niños de origen latinoamericano residentes en España: Un estudio exploratorio, Pre-doctoral dissertation, Universidad Autónoma de Madrid.

Gómez-Berrocal, C. and Navas, M. (2000) Predictores del prejuicio manifiesto y sutil hacia los gitanos, *Revista de Psicología Social*, 15. pp 3-30.

Gómez-Berrocal, C. and Ruiz, J. (2001) Los valores: una construcción cultural asociada al prejuicio hacia los gitanos, inmigrantes y minusválidos. Determinantes sociales del prejuicio étnico, *Revista de Psicología General y Aplicada*, 54. pp 313-329.

Gottmann, J. (1952) *La politique des Etats et leur géographie*. Paris: Colin.

Graham, B. (1998) *Modern Europe: place, culture and identity*. London: Arnold.

Greenberg, B. S., Brand, J. E. and Kósa, É. (1993) *Young people and their orientation to mass media: An International study*. Lansing MI: Michigan State University.

Greenfield, P. M. (1984) *Mind and media. The effects of television, computers and video-games*. London: Fontana.

Grob, A. and Flammer, A. (1999) Macrosocial context and adolescents' perceived control. in: Alsaker, F. D. and Flammer, A. (eds) *The Adolescent experience: European and American adolescents in the 1990s*. Mahwah, NJ: Erlbaum.

Grob, A., Little, T. D., Wanner, B. and Wearing, A. J. (1996) Adolescents' well-being and perceived control across fourteen sociocultural contexts. *Journal of Personality and Social Psychology,* 71, pp 785-795.

Guerrero, S. (2003) Comprensión y detección de claves étnico-raciales en la categorización social: Un estudio con niños de 3 a 5 años, Unpublished pre-doctoral dissertation, Universidad Complutense de Madrid.

Gungwu, W. (1998) Introduction: Migration and New National Identities, in Sinn, E. (ed) *The Last Half Century of Chinese Overseas*. Hong Kong: Hong Kong University Press.

Hackbarth, S. (1997) Web-Based Learning Activities for Children, in Khan, B. (ed) *Web-based instruction*. Englewood Cliffs NY: Educational Technology Publications. pp 191-203.

Hall, S. (1992) New Ethnicities, in Donald, J. and Rattansi, A. (eds), *'Race', Culture and Difference*. London: Sage.

Hall, S. (1996) Introduction: Who needs 'identity'?, in Hall, S. and du Gay, P. (eds) *Questions of Cultural Identity*. London: Sage.

Harvey D. (1989) *The condition of postmodernity: an enquiry into the origins of cultural change*. Oxford: Blackwell.

Havighurst, R. J. (1972) *Developmental tasks and education*. 3rd edition. New York NY: David McKay.

Henley, J. (2003) France to ban pupils' religious dress: outlawing headscarves at school is persecution say Muslims, *The Guardian*, 12 December 2003.

Hesse, B. (2000) *Un/settled Multiculturalisms. Diasporas, Entanglements, Transruptions*. New York: Zed Books.

Hiro, D. (1991) *Black British, White British*. London: Grafton.

Hobsbawm, E. and Ranger, T. (eds) (1982) *The invention of Tradition*. Cambridge: Cambidge University Press.

Hofshire, L. and Greenberg, B. S. (2002) The Media's impact on adolescents' body dissatisfaction, in Brown, J. and Steele, J. (eds) *Sexual teens, sexual media*. Hillsdale, NJ: Lawrence Erlbaum.

Hogan, M. J. (2001) Parents and other adults. models and monitors of healthy media habits, in Singer, D. and Singer, J. (eds) *Handbook of children and the media*. New York NY: Sage Publications. pp 663-680.

Hollinger, D. A. (1995) *Postethnic America: beyond multiculturalism*, New York NY: Basicbooks.

Home Affairs Committee (1985) *Chinese Community in Britain, Second Report from the Home Affairs Committee, Sessions 1984-5, Vol 1*. London: HMSO.

Huntemann, N. and Morgan, M. (2001) Mass media and identity development, in Singer, D. and Singer, J. (eds) *Handbook of children and the media*. New York NY: Sage Publications. pp 309-323.

Hunyady, G. (2002) Psychology of contraselection. *Applied Psychology in Hungary*. 2001/2002. (3-4) pp 7-31.

Hutnik, N. (1991) *Ethnic Minority Identity: A Social Psychological Perspective*. Oxford: Clarendon Press.

Ibsen, H. (1875) *Peer Gynt* (1998 ed) Oxford: Oxford University Press.

Jensen Arnett, J. (2002) The psychology of globalization. *American Psychologist*, 57, (10). pp774-783.

Jensen, R. (1999) *The Dream Society*. New York NY: McGrawHill.

Johnsson-Smaragdi, U. (1983) *TV use and social interaction in adolescence. A longitudinal study*. Stockholm: Almquist and Wiksell.

Joinson, A. (1998) Causes and Implications of Disinhibited Behavior on the Internet, in Gackenbach, J. (ed) *Psychology and the Internet, intrapersonal, interpersonal, and transpersonal implications*. San Diego CA: Academic Press.

Jones, R. (1999) *Teaching Racism or Tackling it*. Stoke-on-Trent: Trentham.

Jost, J. T. and Banaji, M. R. (1994) The role of stereotyping in system-justification and the production of false consciousness. *British Journal of Social Psychology*. 33(1) pp 1-27.

Jülisch, B. R., Sydow, H. and Wagner, C. (1994) Zukunftsvorstellungen Ost- und Westberliner Schüler, in Trommsdorff, G. (ed.) *Psychologische Aspekte des sozio-politischen Wandels in Ostdeutschland*. Berlin: Walter de Gruyter.

Kagitcibasi, C. (2004) Modernization does not mean Westernization: Emergence of a different pattern, in Friedlmeier, W. (ed.) *Culture and Human Development*

Kasurinen, H. (2000) The personal future. General apsects of adolescents' future orientation, in Puuronen, V., Sinisalo, P., Miljukova, I., and Shvets, L. (eds) *Everyday Life and Political Culture of Youth in Karelia. Youth in a Changing Karelia. A comparative study of everyday life, future orientations and political culture of youth in North-West Russia and Eastern Finland*. Aldershot: Ashgate.

Khan, S. (1998) Muslim women: negotiations in the third space, *Signs: Journal of Women in Culture*, 23, 2. pp 463-495.

Kiesler, S., Siegel, J. and McGuire, T. W. (1984) Social psychological aspects of computer-mediated communication, *American Psychologist*, 39. pp 1123-1134.

Killen, M. and Stangor, H. (2001) Children's social reasoning about inclusion and exclusion in gender and race peer groups context, *Child Development,* 72. pp 174-186.

Killen, M., Lee-Kim, J., McGlothin, H. and Stangor, C. (2002) How children and adolescents evaluate gender and racial exclusion, *Monographs of the Society for Research in Child Development,* 67, 271.

Kósa, É. (2002) Effects of TV on adolescents' socialisation process, *Applied Psychology in Hungary,* 3-4 (2001-2002) pp 97-121.

Koselleck, R. (1979) *Vergangene Zukunft, Zur Semantik geschichtlicher Zeiten.* Frankfurt am Main: Suhrkampf.

Kraut, R. E. and Streeter, L. A. (1995) Coordination in software development, *Communication of the ACM,* 38(3) pp 69-81.

Lancaster, K. (ed) (1991) *Modern Consumer Theory.* Aldershot: Elgar.

Larson, R. W. (2002) Globalization, Societal Change, and New Technologies: What they mean for the future adolescence, in Larson, R. W., Brown, B. B. and Mortimer, J. T. (eds) *Adolescents' preparation for the future: Perils and Promise.* Ann Arbor MI: The Society for Research on Adolescence.

Lastrucci, E. (2000) History consciousness, social/political identity and European citizenship, in Ross, A. (ed) *Developing identitiesin Europe.* London: CiCe.

Lastrucci, E. (2002) Youth and European identity, in Näsman, E. and Ross, A. (eds) *Children's Understanding in the New Europe.* Stoke on Trent: Trentham.

László, M. (1999) Példa-kép: A tizenéves korosztály értékválasztásai és a média. *Jel-Kép,* 1993/3. pp 33-49.

Laurin, S. and Klein, J. L. (1999) *L'éducation géographique formation du citoyen et conscience territoriale.* Sainte-Foy : Presses de l'Université du Québec.

Lautier, N. (1997) *Á la rencontre de l'histoire.* Lille: Septentrion presses universitaires

Lenoir, Y. (2002) Les réformes actuelles de la formation à l'enseignement en France et aux Etats-Unis : éléments de mise en perspective socio-historique à partir du concept d'éducation, in *Revue Suisse des Sciences de l'éducation,* 24, (1). pp 91-126.

Lerner, M., Miller, J., and Dale, T. (1978) Just world research and the attribution process: Looking back and ahead. *Psychological Bulletin.* 85, (5), pp 1030-1051.

Lewis, P. (2001) *Between Lord Ahmed and Ali G: Which future for British Muslims?* Report submitted to the Bradford Race Review, chaired by Sir Herman Ouseley. Bradford: Bradford Council.

Leyens, J. P., Yzerbyt, V. and Schadron, G. (1994) *Stereotypes and social cognitio.* London: Sage.

Livingstone, S. (2002) *Young people and new media.* New York NY: Sage.

Mac an Ghaill, M. (1988) *Young, Gifted and Black.* Milton Keynes: Open University Press.

Mac an Ghaill, M. (1994) *The Making of Men.* Buckingham: Open University Press.

Maccoby, E. E. and Martin, J. A. (1983) Socialisation in the context of the family: Parent-child interaction, in: Mussen, P. H. (ed) *Handbook of child psychology.* Vol. IV. John Wiley. pp1-103.

Macdonald, S. (2000) *Approaches to European historical consciousness, reflections and provocations.* Hamburg: Körber Stiftung.

Macek, P. (2003) Everyday life experiences and perceptions of social changes among Czech adolescents: an international comparison. Paper presented at the 6th Regional Congress of the IACCP, Budapest. July 12-16.

Macek, P., Flanagan, C., Gallay, L., Kostron, L., Botcheva, L., and Csapo, B. (1998) Post-communist societies in times of transition: perceptions of change among adolescents in central and eastern Europe. *Journal of Social Issues.* 54(3) pp 547-556.

Macek, P. and Osecká, L. (1996) Importance of adolescents' selves. *Personality and Individual Differences.* 21, 6, pp1021-1027.

Martin Serrano, M. and Velarde, O. (2001) *Informe juventud en España 2000.* Madrid: Instituto de Trabajo y Asuntos Sociales.

Martineau, R. (2000) *L'histoire à l'école, matière à penser.* Paris-Montréal: L'Harmattan.

Mašek, J. (2001) The Impact of Mediated Communication on Children's Identity and Citizenship, in Ross, A. (ed) *Learning for a Democratic Europe.* London: CiCe publication. pp 321-329.

Mašek, J. (2002) Citizenship Education: The Role of Media Environments in Active Learning, in Ross, A. (ed) *Future Citizens in Europe.* London: CiCe. pp 181-186.

Mateju, P. (2003) Trust and Reciprocity Networks: two distinctive dimensions of social capital. Paper presented at the Workshop on Social Capital Measurement. OECD Conference, Budapest.

Mauss, M. (1985) A category of the human mind: the notion of person; the notion of self; translated by W. D. Halls, in *The Category of the Person: anthropology, philosophy, history.* New York: Cambridge University Press.

Mead, M. (1928) (reprinted 1971) *Coming of Age in Samoa: A Psychological Study of Primitive Youth for Western Civilization.* New York: Quill.

Merrill, P. F., Hammons, K., Tolman, M. N., Christensen, L., Vincent, B. R. and Reynolds, P. L. (1992) *Computers in Education,* 2nd edition. Boston MA: Allyn and Bacon.

Miller, D. (1995) *Acknowledging Consumption.* London: Routledge .

Mirza, H. (1992) *Young, Female and Black.* London: Routledge.

Mlicki, P.P. and Ellmers, N. (1996) Being different or being better? National stereotypes and identifications of Polish and Dutch students. *European Journal of Social Psychology.* 26. pp 97-114.

Modood, T. (1992) *Not Easy Being British.* Stoke-on-Trent: Trentham.

Molero, B. (1999) *El proceso de construcción infantil de la identidad nacional: conocimiento del propio país y de los símbolos nacionales.* Bilbao: Servicio editorial de la UPV/EHU.

Moral, F. and Mateos, A. (1999) *La identidad nacional de los jóvenes y el Estado de las Autonomías.* Madrid: Centro de Investigaciones Sociológicas.

Musen, P. H. (ed) (1988) *Handbook of Child Psychology,* 4th edition. New York NY: Wiley.

Nayak, A. (2001) 'Ice White and Ordinary': New perspectives on ethnicity, gender and youth cultural identities, in Francis B. and Skelton, C. (eds) *Investigating Gender: Contemporary Perspectives in Education.* Buckingham: Open University Press.

Nesdale, D. (2001) The development of prejudice in children, in Augoustinos, M. and Reynolds, K. (eds) *Understanding prejudice, racism and social conflict.* London: Sage.

Nesdale, D. and Flesser, D. (2001) Social identity and the development of children's group attitudes, *Child Development,* 72. pp 506-517.

Niesyto, H. and Buckingham, D. (2001) VideoCulture: an introduction, *Journal of Educational Media,* 26(3) pp 167-172.

Noack, P., Hofer, M., Kracke, B. and Klein-Allerman, E. (1995) Adolescents and their parents facing social change: Families in East and West Germany after unification, in Noack, P. Hofer, M. and Youniss, J. (eds) *Psychological Responses to Social Change.* Berlin: de Gruyter.

Noack, P., Karcke, B., Wild, E. and Hofer, M. (2001) Subjective Experiences of Social Change in East and West Germany. *American Behavioral Scientist.* 44(9) pp 1798-1817.

Nogué, J. and Vicente, J. (2001) *Geopolítica, identidad y globalización.* Barcelona: Ed Ariel.

Nurmi, J. E. (1998) (ed) *Adolescents, cultures, conflicts. Growing up in contemporary Europe.* New York NY: Garland Publishing Inc.

OECD (2001) *Background paper on Information and Consumer Decision-Making for sustainable consumption.* Paris: OECD.

Oettingen, G., Little, T.D., Lindenberger, U. and Baltes, P.B. (1994) Causality, agency, and control beliefs in East versus West Berlin children: A natural experiment on the role of context. *Journal of Personality and Social Psychology,* 66, pp 579-595.

Orizo, F.A.and Elzo, J. (2000) *España 2000, entre el localismo y la globalidad.* Madrid: Fundación Santa María y Universidad de Deusto.

Orizo, F.A.and Roque, M.A. (2001) *Cataluña 2001. Los catalanes en la encuesta europea de valores.* Madrid: Fundación Santa María.

Oswald, H., and Krappman, L. (1995) Social life of children in a former bipartite city, in Noack, P. Hofer, M. and Youniss, J. (eds.) *Psychological Responses to Social Change.* Berlin: de Gruyter.

Owen, D. (1994) *Chinese People and 'Other' Ethnic Minorities in Great Britain: Social and Economic Circumstances.* Warwick: Centre for Research in Ethnic Relations, University of Warwick.

Pang M. (1999) The employment situation of young Chinese adults in the British labour market, *Personnel Review*, 28. pp 41-57.

Papoulia-Tzelepi, P, Hegstrup, P. and Ross, A. (eds) (2005) *Emerging identities among Young Children: European Issues.* Stoke on Trent: Trentham.

Paradela, I. (in preparation) Conocimientos de los estereotipos y creencias personales sobre distintas minorías por parte de niños latinoamericanos y españoles de la Comunidad de Madrid, Doctoral dissertation, Universidad Autónoma de Madrid.

Parke, R. D. and Buriel, R. (1998) Socialisation in the family: ethnic and ecological perspectives, in Damon, W. (ed) *Handbook of child psychology,* Vol.III. New York NY: Wiley. pp 463-553.

Parker, D. (1998) Emerging British Chinese Identities: Issues and Problems, in Sinn E. (ed) *The Last Half Century of Chinese Overseas.* Hong Kong: Hong Kong University Press.

Parker, D. (2000) The Chinese Takeaway and the Diasporic Habitus: Space, time and power geometrics, in Hesse B. (ed) *Un/settled Multiculturalisms* London: Zed Books.

Parker, J. (2001) *Structuration.* Buckingham, Open University Press.

Percheron, A. (1993) *La socialisation politique.* Paris: Armand Colin.

Perez, C. (2004) Optimizmus-pesszimizmus kultúrközi összehasonlító vizsgálat magyar és kolumbiai egyetemsiták körében (Optimism and pessimism: cross-cultural comparison between Hungarian and Columbian university students). *Pszichológia.* 24(1) pp 3-35.

Phinney, J. (1990) Ethnic Identity and Adolescents and Adults: Review of Research, *Psychological Bulletin,* 108(3) pp 494-514.

Phinney, J. and Alipuria, L. (1990) Ethnic identity in college students from four ethnic groups, *Journal of Adolescence,* 13(2) pp 171-183.

Pieke, F. (1998) Introduction, in Benton G. and Pieke, F. (eds) *The Chinese in Europe.* Macmillan: Basingstoke.

Pinquart, M. and Silbereisen, R.K. (2004) Human development in times of social change: Theoretical considerations and research needs. *International Journal of Behavioral Development,* 28, (4), pp 289-298.

Puuroenen, V. and Kasurinen, H. (2000) The everyday life of young people in Karelia in the mid-1990, in Puuronen, V., Sinisalo, P., Miljukova, I., and Shvets, L. (eds) *Everyday Life and Political Culture of Youth in Karelia. Youth in a Changing Karelia. A comparative study of everyday life, future orientations and political culture of youth in North-West Russia and Eastern Finland.* Aldershot: Ashgate Ashgate.

Ramsey, P. (1991) The salience of race in young children growing up in an all-white community, *Journal of Educational Psychology,* 83. pp 28-34.

Rattansi, A. (1992) Changing the subject? Racism, culture and education, in J. Donald and Rattansi, A. (ed) *Race, Culture and Difference.* London: Sage.

Reay, D. (2001) 'Spice Girls', 'Nice Girls', 'Girlies' and Tomboys: Gender discourses, girls' cultures and femininities in the primary classroom, *Gender and Education,* 13(2) pp 153-166.

Reid, E. (1999) Language education for multicultural societies, in Ross, A. (ed) *Young Citizens in Europe.* London: CiCe.

Reisman, D. (1950) *The Lonely Crowd: A study of the changing of the American character,* New Haven MA, Yale University Press.

Reitzle, M, and Silbereisen, R.K. (2000) Adapting to Social Change: Adolescent values in eastern and western Germany, in Bynner, J. and Silbereisen, R. K. (eds) *Adversity and Challenge in life in the new Germany and in England.* London: Macmillan.

Rippl, S. and Boehnke, K. (1995) Authoritarianism: Adolescents from East and West Germany and the United States compared, in Youniss, J. (ed) *New Directions for Child Development. After the Wall: Family Adaptations in East and West Germany.* San Francisco CA: Jossey Bass.

Roberts, D. F. and Maccoby, N. (1985) Effects of mass communication, in Lindzey, G. and Aronson, E. (eds) *Handbook of social psychology Vol.1* (2nd edition). New York NY: Random House. pp539-598.

Roberts, K., Clark, S.C., Fagan, C. and Tholen, J. (2000) *Surviving Post-communism. Young people in the former Soviet Union.* Northampton: Edward Elgar Publishing.

Robertson, R. (1995) *Globalisation: social theory and global culture.* London: Sage.

Robinson, J., Witenberg, R. and Sanson, A. (2001) The socialisation of tolerance, in Augoustinos M. and Reynolds, K. (eds) *Understanding prejudice, racism, and social conflict.* London: Sage.

Roland-Lévy, C. and Ross, A. (eds) (2003) *Political learning and Citizenship in Europe.* Stoke on Trent: Trentham.

Rorty, R. (1989) *Contingency, Irony and Solidarity.* Cambridge: Cambridge University Press.

Rosengren, K. E. (ed) (1994) *Media effects and beyond. Culture, socialization and lifestyles.* Routledge: London and New York.

Rosengren, K. E. and Windahl, S. (1989) *Media Matter: TV use in childhood and adolescence.* Norwood NJ: Ablex.

Royle, E. (ed) (1998) *Issues of regional identity: In honour of John Marshall.* Manchester: Manchester University Press.

Rubin, K. H., Bukowski, W. and Parker, J. G. (1998) Peer interactions, relationships, and groups, in: Damon, W. (ed) *Handbook of child psychology,* Vol. III. New York NY: John Wiley. pp 619-701.

Ruiz Jiménez, A. M. (2003) *¿Y tu de quien eres? Identidad europea y lealtad a la nación.* Madrid: UNED.

Rushdie, S. (1988) *The Satanic Verses.* London: Jonathan Cape.

Rutland, A. (1999) The development of national prejudice, in-group favouritism and self-stereotypes in British children, *British Journal of Social Psychology,* 38. pp 55-70.

Rutter, J. (2001) *Supporting refugee children in 21st century Britain: a compendium of essential information.* Stoke on Trent: Trentham.

Saraswathi, T. S. and Larson, R. (2002). Adolescence in the global perspective : An agenda for social policy. in Brown, B., Larson, R. and Saraswathi, T. (eds.) *The World's Youth: Adolescence in Eight Regions of the World.* New York: Cambridge University Press.

Saris, W. E. and Ferligoj, A. (1995) Life satisfaction and domain satisfaction in ten European countries: correlation at the individual level, in Saris, W., Veenhoven, R., Scherpenzeel, A. and Bunting, B. (eds) *A comparative study of satisfaction with life in Europe.* Budapest: Eötvös University Press.

Sassen, S. (1996) *Losing control? Sovereignty in an age of globalisation.* New York NY: Columbia University Press.

Scarr, S., Weinberg, R. A. and Levine, A. (1983) *Understanding development.* New York NY: Harcourt Brace Jovanovich.

Schlegel, A. (2000) The global spread of adolescent culture, in Crockett, L. J. and Silbereisen, R. K. (eds) *Negotiating adolescence in times of social change.* Cambridge: Cambridge University Press.

Selwyn, N. (2002) *Literature Review in Citizenship, Technology and Learning. Report 3*: Nesta Fturelab Series. available on: http://www.nestafuturelab.org/research/reviews/cit04.htm.

Sewell, T. (1997) *Black Maculinities and Schooling: How black boys survive modern schooling.* Stoke on Trent: Trentham.

Shain, F. (2003) *The Schooling and Identity of Asian Girls.* Stoke on Trent: Trentham.

Sham, S. and Woodrow, D. (1998) Chinese children and their families in England, *Research Papers in Education,* 13(2) pp 203-226.

Shotsberger, P. G. (2000) The Human Touch: Synchronous Communication in Web-Based Learning, *Educational Technology,* 40(1) pp 40-44.

Shotsberger, P. G. (1997) Emerging roles for instructors and learners in the WBI classroom, in Khan, B. (ed) *Web-based instruction.* Englewood Cliffs NY: Educational Technology Publications. pp 101-106.

Signorelli, N. (2001) Television's gender role images and contribution to stereotyping, in Singer, D. and Singer, J. (eds) *Handbook of Children and the Media.* New York NY: Sage. pp 341-358.

Silbereisen, R. K., and Youniss, J. (2001) Family and development in childhood and adolescence: Germany before and after reunification. *American Behavioral Scientist.* 44.

Singer, D. G. and Singer, J. L. (eds) (2001) *Handbook of Children and the Media.* New York NY: Sage Publications.

Sinisalo, P., Shvets, L. and Rusanova, V. (2000) Value orientations of Russian and Finnish young people in Puuronen, V., Sinisalo, P., Miljukova, I., and Shvets, L. (eds) *Everyday Life and Political Culture of Youth in Karelia. Youth in a Changing Karelia. A comparative study of everyday life, future orientations and political culture of youth in North-West Russia and Eastern Finland.* Aldershot: Ashgate Ashgate 2000.

Siraj-Blatchford, I. (ed.) (1993) *'Race', Gender and the Education of Teachers.* Buckingham: Open University Press.

Šmahel, D. (2003) *Psychologie a Internet.* Praha: Triton.

Smith, P.B., Dugan, S. and Trompenaars, F. (1996) National culture and the values of organizational employees. *Journal of Cross-Cultural Psychology.* 27. pp 231-264.

Song, M. (1997) 'You're Becoming More and More English': Investigating Chinese siblings' cultural identities, *New Community,* 23(3) pp 343-362.

Steffens, H. (2002) Consumer citizenship-responsible interaction with the market?' in Thoresen, V. (ed) *Developing Consumer Citizenship,* Conference Proceedings, Hamar: Hedmark College.

Sternberg, E. (1999) *The Economy of Icons: How Business Manufactures Meaning.* Westport, CO: Praeger.

Suler, J. R. (1998) Adolescents in cyberspace: The good, the bad, and the ugly, in *The Psychology of Cyberspace,* available on: http://www.rider.edu/suler/psycyber/adoles.html.

Suler, J. R. (2000) Case studies and the evolution of digital life forms, *CyberPsychology and Behavior,* 3. pp 219-220.

Sverko, B. (1999) The Work Importance Study: Recent Changes in Values in Croatia. *Applied Psychology: An International Review.* 48. pp 89-102.

Swartz, J. D. and Hatcher, T. (1996) Virtual Experience: The Impact of Mediated Communication in a Democratic Society, *Educational Technology,* 36(6) pp 40-44.

Sydow, H., Wagner, C., Jülisch, B.R., Kauf, H. (1999) Future oriented control and subjective well-being of students in East and West Berlin, in Silbereisen, R. K. and von Eye, A. (eds) *Growing up in Times of Social Change.* Berlin: Walter de Gruyter. 107-130.

Tajfel, H. and Turner, J.C. (1979) An integrative theory of intergroup conflict, in Austin W, and Worchel, S. (eds) *The social psychology of intergroup relations.* Monterey, CA: Brooks/Cole.

Tam, S. K. (1998) Representations of 'the Chinese' and 'Ethnicity' in British Racial Discourse, in Sinn, E. (ed) *The Last Half Century of Chinese Overseas.* Hong Kong: Hong Kong University Press.

Taylor, M. (1987) *Chinese Pupils in Britain.* Berkshire: NFER-Nelson.

Teacher Training Agency (TTA) (2003) *Survey of NQTs 2003.* London: Teacher Training Agency.

Thoresen, V. (2002) *Consumer citizenship-global democracy in a commercial context?* Hedmark: Hedmark University College.

Tierney, R., Kieffer, R., Stowell, L., Desai, L., Whalin, K. and Moss, A. (1992) *Computer acquisition: a longitudinal study of the influence of high computer access on students thinking, learning and interactions.* Cupertino, CA: Apple Computer Inc.

Titarenko, L. (1995) The value orientation of Belarus Youth, in Riordan, J., Williams, C. and Ilynsky, I. (eds) *Young people in post-communist Russia and Eastern Europe.* Aldershot: Dartmouth Publishing.

Topalova, V. (2003) Changing values and identities of the Bulgarian young people: a cross-cultural perspective. Paper presented at the 6th Regional Congress of the IACCP. Budapest. July 12-16.

Trommsdorff, G. (1994) Future time perspective and control orientation: Social conditions and consequences, in Zaleski, Z. (ed) *Psychology of Future Orientation.* Lublin: Towarzystvo Naukowe KUI.

Trommsdorff, G. (1999) Social Change and Individual Development in East Germany: A Methodological Critique in Silbereisen, R. K. and von Eye, A. (eds) *Growing up in Times of Social Change.* Berlin: Walter de Gruyter.

Turiel, E. (1983) *The development of social knowledge: Morality and convention.* Cambridge: Cambridge University Press.

Turkle, S. (1988) *Life on the screen.* New York: Touchstone Books

Turner, J. (1987) Rediscovering the social group, in Turner, J. Hogg, M. Oakes, P., Reicher, S. and Wetherell, M. (eds) *Rediscovering the social group: A self-categorisation theory.* Oxford: Blackwell.

Tutiaux-Guillon, N. (1998, 2000) L'enseignement de l'histoire sociale en collège et en lycée, l'exemple de la société d'Ancien régime et de la société du XIXe siècle, Universite Paris 7-Denis Diderot, 1998; edited Lille, thèses à la carte 2000.

Tutiaux-Guillon, N. (2000) *L'Europe entre projet politique et objet scolaire.* Paris : INRP.

Tutiaux-Guillon, N. (2001) French school history: resistance to debates and controversial issue, in Pellens, K. *et al.* (eds) *Historical consciousness and history teaching in a globalizing society.* Frankfurt: Peter Lang. pp 39-50.

Tutiaux-Guillon, N. (2003a) L'histoire enseignée entre coutume disciplinaire et formation de la conscience historique, in Tuttiaux-Guillon, N. and Nourisson, D. (eds) *Identités, mémoires, conscience historique.* Saint-Etienne: Publications de l'Université de Saint-Etienne. p 27-41.

Tutiaux-Guillon, N. (2003b) Teaching history for Europe?, in Koerber, A. (ed) *Geschichte – Leben – Lernen.* Schwalbach: Wochenschau.

Tutiaux-Guillon, N. *et al.* (2004) Research in progress: 'Les finalités dans l'enseignement de l'histoire-géographie: des intentions aux pratiques à l'école et au collège' [Taking account of the civic and social aims of history and geography teaching], directed by Tutiaux-Guillon, will be on the site of the IUFM of Lyon: www.lyon.iufm.fr/recherche.

Tutiaux-Guillon, N., and Mousseau M. J. (1998) *Les jeunes et l'histoire.* Paris : INRP.

Uhlendorf, H. (2004) After the Wall: Parental attitudes to child rearing in East and West Germany. *International Journal of Behavioural Development.* 28(1) pp 71-82.

UNDP (United Nations Development Program) (1998) *Human Development Report.* Oxford: Oxford University Press.

UNEP (2001) *Consumption Opportunities.* Geneva: UNEP.

van den Auweele, Y. (1975) Zukunftsvorstellungen von 15 jährigen in der DDR und der BRD, *Kölner Zeitschrift für Soziologie und Sozialpsychologie,* 27, pp 592-610.

Van Der Leeuw-Roord, (ed) (1998) *The state of history education in Europe, challenges and implications of the Youth and History survey.* Hamburg: Körber-Stiftung.

Van Hoorn, J. L., Komlósi, Á., Suchar, E. and Samelson, D. A. (2000) *Adolescent Development and Rapid Social Change.* Albany NY: State University of New York Press.

Vari-Szilágyi, I. and Solymosi, Z. (1999) *A siker lélektana (The psychology of success),* Budapest: Hatodik Síp Alapítvány. Új Mandátum Könyvkiadó.

Verkuyten, M. (2001) National identification and intergroup evaluations in Dutch children, *British Journal of Developmental Psychology,* 19. pp 559-571.

Verkuyten, M. (2002) Perceptions of ethnic discrimination by minority and majority early adolescents in the Netherlands, *International Journal of Psychology,* 37. pp 321-332.

Verma, G., Zec, P. and Skinner, G. (1994) *The Ethnic Crucible: Harmony and Hostility in Multi-Ethnic Schools.* London: Falmer.

Villanueva, M. (2004) Fronteras, identidades y diversidad: un ejercicio de re-lectura del mapa político europeo. *Enseñanza de las Ciencias Sociales.* 3. pp 103-110.

Walper, S. and Silbereisen, R.K. (1994) Economic hardship in Polish and German families. Some consequences for adolescents, in Silbereisen, R. K. and Todt, E. (eds) *Adolescence in Context.* New York NY: Springer Verlag..

Watson, J. (1977) The Chinese: Hong Kong Villagers in the British Catering Trade, in Watson J. (ed) *Between Two Cultures.* Oxford: Basil Blackwell. pp 181-213.

Weber, M. (1983) *Max Weber on capitalism, bureaucracy and religion*, London: Allen and Unwin.

Westwood, S. (1990) Racism, black masculinity and the politics of space, in Morgan J. and Hearn, D. (eds), *Men, Masculinities and Social Theory*. London: Unwin Hyman.

Wetherell, M. (1993) *Masculinity as constructed reality. Paper at conference on constructed realities: Therapy, theory and research*, Lofoten, Norway, June.

Whitehead, S. (2002) *Men and Masculinities*. Cambridge: Polity Press.

Wiesenberg, F. and Hutton, S. (1996) Teaching a graduate program using computer-mediated conferencing software. *Journal of Distance Education*, 11(1) pp 83-100.

Wilkomirska, A, Dolata, R. and Fraczek, A. (2000) The relationship between school democracy and trust in state institutions among Polish teenagers. Paper presented at the 7th Biennial Conference of the European Association for Research on Adolescence, Jena.

Wober, J. M. (1986) The lens of television and the prism of personality, in Bryant, J. and Zillman, D. (eds) *Perspectives on media effects*. Hillsdale, NJ: Lawrence Erlbaum. pp 205-233.

Wong, L. (1994) Di(s)-secting and Dis(s)-closing 'Whiteness', *Feminism and Psychology*, 4, (1). pp 133-153.

Woodrow, D. and Sham, S. (2001) Chinese Pupils and their Learning Preferences, *Race, Ethnicity and Education*, 4(4) pp 377-394.

World Health Organisation (2003) *WHO statistics*, http://www.who.org.

Yordanova, L. (1995) Youth beliefs and values in Bulgaria, in Riordan, J., Williams, C. and Ilynsky, I. (eds) *Young people in post-communist Russia and Eastern Europe*. Aldershot: Dartmouth Publishing.

Index

Advertising 159
agency 6, 24
Archer, L. 5, 55-69, 165
Asian culture 57
assimilation 57

Basque country 49, 50

Catalonia 45, 51-2
chat rooms 145-7
Chinese
    culture 75
    identity 78, 83
    in Europe 72
    Chinese-British 71-87
citizenship 17, 149-51
commercialisation 155,
    159-160
communication
    technologies 138-141
community 18
competition 28-32, 34
consumer
    citizenship 162-3
    identity 6, 153-164
cosmopolitanism 47
culture
    difference 13, 14, 38,
    57, 64
    identity 43

dependency 23
discrimination 55, 62, 92,
    91-2

Enesco, I. 5, 89-101, 165
enterprise 23, 27
ethnicity 5, 7, 41, 45, 55-7,
    71-3
    prejudice 92-4, 95,
    98-100
    minority education 55,
    57, 87 fn

Europe
    changes in East 4, 12
    East and West 3, 11,
    36-7
    identity 1, 4, 9, 135-6
European Union 13

family 20-21
feminism 59-60
France 109-120
Francis, B. 5, 71-87, 105
Fülöp, M. 5, 1-10, 11-41,
    165

gender 85, 125, 125-6
geography curriculum 3, 10,
    103-4, 109-110
German reunification 15,
    21, 26, 35, 37
global identity 2
global production 157
globalisation 6, 7
glocalisation 8, 42
goals 25, 36, 81
Great Britain 55-69, 71-87
Gypsies 96-8, 99-100

Health 126, 161
hijab 56, 61-2
historical consciousness
    105-6, 114-5
history 3, 10, 103-120
    curriculum 109-110
    teaching 103-4
    student perceptions
    111-3
Hungary 130, 131
hypermedia 141

identity 108-9
individualism 17, 19, 37
individualism-collectivism
    16-9

Islamophobia 55, 62

Kósa, E. 6, 121-136, 166

linguistic identity 44, 45,
    49, 53
localisation 6, 45-7

Maiztegui Onate, C. 5, 7,
    41-54, 166
market economy 29-30
Masek, J. 6, 137-151, 167
media 6, 121-136
    new 137-151
    role models 123-4
    use of 128-131
migration 44
minorities in media 126
money 158
moral code 30-3, 34
multimodality 139-141
multiple identity 8, 9, 42,
    58, 68-9, 80
Muslims 55-69
    boys 62-8
    girls 58-62

Navarro Sava, A. 5, 89-101,
    165

planning 25
post-socialism 13
prejudice 89-92

religion 7, 55
republicanism 109
Ross, A. 1-10, 167

Salman Rushdie 55, 63, 65,
    69 fn
separatedness 19-22
sexism 66-7

social change 1, 4, 11, 26, 7, 153
social exclusion 9
social identity 1, 6
socialisation 121-4, 153
Spain 41-54, 95-101
state sovereignty 41, 43
stereotypes 89-90
Sweden 132-3
symbolic identity 156

territoriality 42-50
consciousness 106-7
Thorensen, V. 6, 9, 153-164, 167
tolerance 94, 95-101
transitional societies 16
trust/distrust 22-3
Tutiaux Guillon, N. 3, 9, 103-120, 167

Villanueva, M. 5, 7, 41-54, 167

web-culture 142-3
western identity 2, 7
work roles 127

youth culture 7, 76-7, 121-5

CL

305.
235
094
GRO